D0127463

Lesley + Jonathan —
Wishing you
much love +

HEART SPARKS *joy +*
ease!

7 Practices

For Loving Your Life

Ruth Davis

359press

FIRST EDITION

Cover art used with permission of the artist, Barbara Bagan

Library of Congress Cataloging-in-Publication Data

Davis, Ruth.

Heart sparks : 7 practices for loving your life / Ruth Davis.

ISBN-13: 978-0692314012 (359Press)

Contents

Introduction

We all have things in our lives - a sudden death, a new baby, chronic pain, a divorce, the new school year, the loss of a job, a near-fatal accident, even just moving to a new house - things happen that shake us up, knock us for a loop, throw us spinning into confusion, and fear and not knowing what's next.

Sometimes the thing that shakes us and wakes us is our own boredom. We aren't challenged at work, we don't engage in anything exciting in our free time. We live our routine, park ourselves in front of our technology and, even though we don't love it, we think that life is fine.

And then something happens and suddenly fine is no longer enough. We know we want to make a change. But we don't even know what else we might want.

Our life is constantly calling us to be bigger. To live with more meaning, more intention, more joy. To share more of our true selves. But it usually takes a big event for us to realize we want to make these changes in our lives.

But really, we have this choice every day - not just when our lives are in crisis.

Every day we get to choose to pause, and breathe. To respond instead of react, to approach with kindness and compassion, first ourselves and then others. Every day we get to choose the life we want to be living.

This book is an invitation for you to step back from the life you are living and discern if it is enough.

To remember what you love. To explore beyond what you think is possible. To see what else you might want for yourself in this lifetime.

My intention is that this book will spark something in you, something deeper in you that you haven't been in touch with for a while. Something that will get you excited. Something that will stir your heart.

We are not encouraged, in this society, to follow our hearts. It's a lot easier to just go to work, take care of the family, and put off your dreams for someday. Until enough time passes that we forget what those dreams are. Or we die or get too old to pursue them.

And that's why I wrote this book -- to help you remember what you love, so you can start living more of it. Now.

This book will guide you through the seven practices for loving your life: Grounding. Quieting. Exploring. Getting Clear. Letting Go. Imagining. Taking Action.

I've included stories about me and some of my coaching clients (their names have been changed for privacy.) And I've included questions and exercises so that you have some structure and jumping off places to do your own exploring.

The chapters are intended to be read in order so that you build on new skills and practices, but if a title jumps out at you, go for it. You can read one new chapter every week for a whole year, or spend an entire month on a single set of questions that really stir something in you.

You can read the book with a group of friends and share your questions and insights. And you can join me and other readers in our online community.

It's up to you.

I know that I always learn the most from the things I resist the most. So notice which questions pull you in and which ones make you want to close the book and run.

And remember, things don't change in a moment.

It is through regular, conscious practice that we open to new thoughts, shift our behaviors and give ourselves permission to take new actions.

I hope these seven practices for loving your life will help you choose and create a life you love.

Prologue: Break and Grow

"Broken hearted often leads to broken open. And broken open is the perfect environment for finding out who you are and why you're here. Break and grow."

- Michele Woodward

On September 16, 2007, emergency open heart surgery saved my life. I didn't have clogged arteries or heart disease. I had a myxoma, a very rare benign tumor that was almost completely blocking the blood flow through the left atrium of my heart.

They discovered it after I had an episode of sharp ice pick stabbing pain in my back and chest and the inability to breathe. And yes, jaw pain and arm pain too.

It started right after dinner out with friends, so I thought it was indigestion. I made a cup of tea and smoked some pot to calm down. And then I just laid in my bed and tried to find a position of least resistance so I could just focus on breathing.

I didn't call 911. I knew that if I went to the ER, that crazy, noisy chaos would kill me. I knew that I just needed to be still and quiet and just breathe through it.

I did call Marika, my ex-partner who is a nurse and was

still my best friend, but she was out with a friend and not answering her phone. By the time she called me back two hours later, all of the symptoms had subsided.

I felt fine in the morning. I worked on my Mac Tips newsletter that I emailed monthly to clients. I did laundry. I read a few more chapters of Harry Potter and the Prisoner of Azkaban.

In the afternoon, Marika took me to Urgent Care, just to be safe. That's where they saw an abnormality in my blood work indicative of a clot. They sent me to the closest ER, the Heart Hospital, for further tests.

They took x-rays. I did a stress test. I could hardly breathe after walking on the treadmill for just a few minutes. We waited for the echo-cardiogram technician to come in and he's the one who found the tumor, nearly encapsulating the left atrium in my heart.

And he told me he was surprised I was still alive.

He said that most people with a myxoma die before it's detected. That it's like a head of broccoli - you can brush your hand across it and small pieces will break off. With the myxoma, small pieces usually break off and cause a blockage some place else in the body and you die of a massive stroke.

I thought about how, just two weeks before, Marika and I were on vacation in Michigan with her mom, and I was climbing to the tops of lighthouses, coughing all the way up and back down. I'd been coughing for years, and assumed it was from so many years of smoking pot. And the fact that I had asthma. But now I knew that I was coughing because not enough oxygen was circulating in my body. And that I could have died.

Marika and I joked about how tricky it would have been to carry my body down those spiraling lighthouse steps. But we didn't talk about me actually dying. I didn't need to. I only wanted to focus on healing.

The idea of having open heart surgery didn't scare me. I knew I'd be fine. I was young, only 48, and pretty healthy if you didn't count the extra fifty pounds I was carrying around. All went well, they removed the 5.5 cm tumor from my heart and six days later I went home to recover.

I had very little energy those first few weeks. I wasn't interested in watching TV. I didn't have the concentration to read or watch a movie. Everything in my world slowed down. I couldn't do much, so I rejoiced in the simplest of things, like being able to open the refrigerator, walk a full circle around the pool, reach the shower massage so that I could take a shower by myself.

I journaled, but not much. I watched a little TV. I doodled with the crayons my mother brought over.

But when you are recovering from open heart surgery, you can't busy yourself with too much doing or distract yourself with a lot of meaningless activities or mindless chatter.

When you are recovering, at first, all you can do is sit. And breathe. And even that is so painful.

Maybe it was the pain that made me so aware of my breathing. And by focusing on my breathing, I was able to stay in the present moment.

I had to let go of what I wished I could be doing and begin focusing on what I could do: breathing, sitting still, saying thank you.

Before the surgery, my life was pretty sweet. I lived in a friend's guest house across the street from a tree-rimmed grassy park. I had a successful Mac computer training business, I went on great beach vacations, I made mixed media art pieces and sold them in galleries. I belonged to a women's spirituality group and facilitated creativity workshops.

Marika and I had split up in 2004 after 14 years together, but we were working through the hard stuff, trying to stay connected. And we were sharing the dogs, Laddy and Mabel.

I loved my little guest house. It was a studio apartment with a full kitchen and bath and a large covered patio. And there was a pocket door in the living space that opened into a 20 x 20 converted garage with 4' x 9' wide windows and a

Saltillo tiled floor.

This was my work space and art making studio. It's where I grieved the end of the relationship, where I had a summer fling, where I learned to dance with tulle and play the cello. The guest house had been a healing space after the break up and now, it was once again, a place for my heart to heal.

But when I moved back in to return to life as I knew it, nothing was the same. I didn't want to make art. I didn't even do much writing. I was still smoking and working, but very little excited me.

I remember just sitting a lot, watching hours of HGTV and the Food network, feeling like I was in a wide open void. While this is typical with recovering heart patients, my biggest fear was that I wasn't ever going to be creative again.

I knew I had to find new ways to tap into my creative self and discover how I wanted to express myself authentically. But I didn't even know what I wanted to say.

I wanted to do more of my "real work," but I had no idea what that was.

And so I was asking myself lots of questions:

What did I really want to do?

What did I want most in my life?

What was holding me back?

How could I best serve others?

9

What brings me real joy?

What were my biggest dreams?

I had no answers. Only questions. And, literally, new space in my heart to explore.

I began saying no to invitations that felt more like obligations. I let go of relationships that drained me. And I became acutely aware of the love and support in my life.

I realized that, what I wanted, more than anything, was more connection in my life. But, being stoned all the time, I was usually too spacey to drive or too tired to go out, and too fixated on feeling good to risk any vulnerability.

And then, there was that day, that moment, when I realized I couldn't have what I truly wanted if I continued to get high. And so I quit. Cold turkey. Just like that.

But I was still so scared to be in my body.

Post surgery, I had seen a cardiologist to follow up, and he said I didn't need cardiac rehab because I was young and otherwise healthy, that I could resume my regular activities. He told me to come back in a year for an echo-cardiogram, just to make sure the tumor wasn't growing back.

I joined my local Curves, a women's workout club, but I got short of breath quickly, just like before the surgery, and I was sure the tumor was growing back. I wore a halter monitor during a workout and it confirmed that my heart rate was where it should be for my age and weight.

Marika assured me that it was just my asthma, and a matter of building up my stamina and strength. But I was terrified.

So I quit Curves and just walked the dogs and continued my weekly yoga practice and that was as much physical activity as I engaged in.

Finally, a year later, a friend encouraged me to ask for a referral for cardiac rehab. She explained that it was more than just exercising - that it was to get me back into my body in a safe and comfortable way. That they would monitor my vitals the whole time. And that they understood about the fear.

My friend also put me in touch with a woman who had similar fears after her own heart surgeries. Talking with someone who really understood what I was feeling and fearing calmed me down.

I signed up for rehab and went three times a week for two months, until I finally understood that I had a healthy heart. That everyone gets short of breath after a lot of exercise. That it's a good thing to sweat, to get my heart rate up, to breathe so deep and hard that I feel my heart beating.

In the seven years since they cracked my ribs open, I have

trained to become a life coach, worked with a high level business coach to up-level my Mac business, and written my first book. I live part of the year in my motor home across the street from the beach in central California and part with family in Phoenix. I work with clients virtually, and lead creativity workshops, women's retreats, and the Living Room Ladies coaching circles.

And I know that these things are happening, that my life has shifted and opened up because I have shifted and opened up. Because I got quiet and I learned how to listen.

I learned that living the questions is more important than knowing the answers. And I learned how to trust my heart.

For more than two years after the surgery, I felt an actual buzzing in the area where I imagined the tumor had been. I remember so clearly, being at my first life-coaching class and we had to walk up to a person we didn't know and stand as close as we felt comfortable. In the exact moment that I was feeling close enough, my heart started buzzing.

And now, all these years later, I still listen in to that space in my heart for my deepest knowing.

And every time I get lost again and forget all of this, I eventually remember to simply pause, and breathe, and start again, at the beginning.

Practice 1:

Grounding

Begin with Being

When I step back and see where I was just a few years ago, it amazes me. To an outsider, I seemed to be living a pretty good life. I had my own Mac training business that supported me and my lifestyle, I lived in a cute guesthouse, I made and sold my art. But I had no idea what my passion was.

I didn't even really know what passion meant. I kept hearing people talk about their dreams, their purpose, their heart's desire, and I felt like a total failure, because I had no idea what that meant for me.

These people were happy. Joyful, even. They laughed a lot. They seemed connected to something bigger than themselves.

And I wanted to be all of that too.

But I had no idea how to get there.

I signed up for a weekend writing workshop taught by a dear friend who always seems to know exactly what I need to hear. She assigned everyone pre-class homework. Mine was to explore the word Being and then make something that was not a piece writing. And then write about it.

I thought about making some wind chimes, or something with water. But they were too simple. Instead I made a deck of cards of things I wanted to BE that started with the letter B. Bountiful. Bendy. Be in my Body. Brave.

I made a few cards at a time, but only while it was relaxing and mindful. As soon as I felt like I was working too hard to come up with another B word, I'd stop and do something else.

Making the deck of cards and then writing about the process was eye-opening. It was so much about sitting in silence, being with whatever came up. And then letting go.

It was the first time I approached a project so aware that I was following the energy of the making. One idea led to another and I even found wallpaper samples of honeycombs and bees that I used for the back of the cards.

Sure, making the deck of cards was a fun kind of being because it revolved around creativity. I did have to work through some judgments and frustrations and limiting beliefs, but overall, the experience was not uncomfortable.

Being with my feelings isn't quite as fun. But it's just as necessary.

Being means just showing up. Being present. It is the willingness to sit with yourself, with your situation and not do anything, but just be with it, be in it. Being means creating a space for yourself. It can be a physical space, a room where you can go and you can close the door and just be with yourself. Being can be creating a time-out for yourself, creating some space in your full-scheduled day for just you.

Have you seen that commercial for a van—the mom takes her time-outs inside the family van in the driveway. There is chaos in the house in the background, but she can't see it. You can see how calm and content and happy she is, because she is able to get away from all of her family responsibilities for just a little while.

We all need this. We need this quiet time for ourselves so that we can simply be.

But being is very uncomfortable for a lot of people. I know it was for me, for a long time.

Because Being brings up feelings. Being offers a place for all of those monkey voices in your head to scream all of your old tapes about unworthiness, laziness, and the whole vocabulary of shoulds.

No wonder we're so much more comfortable when we're doing.

But as we practice being with our thoughts without judging them, just letting go of all of the noise in our heads, we can actually begin to enjoy the quiet.

Because it's in this quiet that we hear things beyond those monkey voices. We begin to notice details. We begin to pay attention to things beyond our ordinary lives.

And I'll tell you something, it's in this quiet that we begin to really hear our heart's desires.

You don't have to be a master meditator and sit cross-legged on the floor for an hour to get quiet. You could just sit and watch the flames of a fire. Or hang a feeder in your yard and spend some time each day watching the birds. Maybe, the next time you are waiting to pick up the kids, instead of getting on the phone, roll the windows down and watch the sky. Pausing, slowing down, being with yourself where you are, is the first step to making changes in your life.

And notice, the letters in being, rearranged, also spell begin.

And so, when you are able to sit with yourself and be more comfortable being, it becomes a place to begin.

 *HEART SPARKS*

Spend a few minutes each day pausing, noticing, just slowing down the pace of your day.

What do you see? What do you notice?

How does it feel?

The Art of Breathing

Most of us are completely unaware of **when** we breathe. Yet breathing is the simplest thing you can do to slow down, get quiet and come to the present moment.

When you are breathing with awareness, you don't feel shame or regret. When you are following your breath, there is no worry about the future. When you are consciously breathing, the only thing you feel is alive.

So take a breath. Really. Right now.. ...just breathe in and out a few times. Become aware of the inhalation, and then the exhalation. Feel what it feels like to breathe in a little bit deeper, all the way into your belly. And then let it out. Let it go.

Most of us are shallow breathers. We breathe high into our chests, not deep into the lower lobes of our lungs.

And yet breathing into our lower lobes activates the calming receptors that reside there. Breathing into our lower lungs stimulates the lymphatic system so that waste products can be efficiently carried from the body. Breathing into the lower lobes allows the rib cage to be elastic and open.

This deep, whole lung breathing, is also called belly

breathing because we can see our bellies rise when we fill our lower lobes with air.

Belly breathing is not hard to do. It requires no special equipment. It just takes practice.

 **HEART SPARKS**

Take a deep, slow breath in.

Pull that breath deep into your belly. And then exhale.

Breathe in again, deep and slow, and this time, when you let it out, make a sound. Any kind of sound - a word, a grunt, a deep sigh. Whatever feels right.

Do this four more times, slowly, deeply, breathing in and out, with sound.

Now close your eyes and just listen to your breath.

If your mind wanders, just re-connect with your breath, following it all the way in and out again.

And bring yourself into a space of nothing. If a thought pops up, acknowledge it and let it go, like a cloud floating by, shifting shapes until it disappears.

And begin to notice the stillness inside of you.

Maybe you can even feel your heartbeat.

It is in this quiet space that you find peace.

And it is in this quiet space where you meet your heart.

In this place of opening, you can ask yourself, what do I need to feel grounded, supported? What do I really need right now. And just listen...without expecting an answer. You are simply allowing the question to be a question, something you're curious about, something that excites you, something you want to know more about.

Notice what comes up. It could be a word, an image, a negative thought that you can't/don't/shouldn't...

Notice it and then let it go with a deep exhalation. And continue to breathe, deep into your lower lobes, full into your belly, in and out.

If you start to fidget in your body, just re-connect with your breath. Sit for a little while longer, and then slowly, allow your breath to return to its natural rhythm.

Imagine if you did this, **practiced this** breathing exercise, for just a few minutes every day. How might you feel differently?

I know for me, this simple act of sitting and breathing continues to be the single most powerful thing I do to reconnect with my heart.

For an audio recording of a breathing meditation, visit http://www.sparktheheart.com/mp3/breathing.mp3

Grounded, Like a Tree

As you start taking those extra minutes to just sit still in your own silence, creating the space to begin noticing your thoughts, your habits, the world outside of yourself…well, not only might it get uncomfortable for you, but there may be people and situations in your life that are uncomfortable with these new behaviors as well.

Your friends and family may not like what you are doing, they may not like the boundaries you are creating, they may resent this time you are claiming for yourself. Or maybe the doubts will come from your own voices- complaining that you have no time for this silliness, that you're too old to follow your heart, that you've tried this kind of thing before and it didn't work.

And so we have to find ways to practice feeling solid in our choices, supported in our uncertainty, grounded in our beliefs. And grounded in our bodies. Every day. Even on the days you feel invincible. So that when the winds of discomfort begin to blow, you will feel rooted, secure, strong, safe, confident in these new choices you are making for yourself.

Breathing is one way to ground and center yourself.

Standing in a strong yoga pose is another. You can take a walk, or plant something in your garden to ground yourself.

Drawing something that can visually remind you of that solid, rooted feeling is also a powerful tool for grounding yourself.

 ***HEART SPARKS***

What you will need:

a minimum of 30 minutes

a quiet, comfortable place to work

blank paper (at least 8x10) or a sketchbook or you can use your
Book of Observations

colors (markers, crayons, colored pencils...)

Stand up and shake yourself loose.

Gently shift your weight from your toes to your heels, settling
evenly, centered between the two.

Feel your feet connected to the ground, as if there are roots
coming out of the soles of your feet, going deep into the earth.

Imagine you are a tree, solidly planted in the ground. Imagine
your roots connecting you to the nutrients in the earth, your
branches reaching into the sky. You can move and sway with
the breeze and even in a big storm, your roots hold you strong
and steady.

What kind of tree are you?

Where are you planted?

What season is it?

Gather your drawing supplies and draw your tree.

Connecting With Your Body

In this fast-paced world of multi-tasking and multi-media, many of us spend more than half our day sitting in front of a computer screen or driving around town, running errands, hauling kids from one activity to another. Often, the only time we pay attention to our bodies is when they hurt.

If we are not using our bodies, we can't move, we can't take action. Because action requires some kind of physical act. Whether it's making a phone call or writing a letter or standing at the edge of the unknown and leaping, action is a physical manifestation of our thoughts.

We have to consciously and constantly connect with our physical bodies if we want to be able to take these actions.

I'm not suggesting you start going to the gym every day or begin training for a marathon. While these are great activities, it's not the kind of body connecting I'm talking about.

I'm talking about body consciousness. Body awareness. Being aware of being in your body.

 *HEART SPARKS*

How often do you get up from your chair and stretch your body, reaching from head to toe, rolling your neck and shoulders, loosening all of the tight spots and tensions?

Do you get massages? Take baths? When's the last time you took a leisurely walk?

This week, do things that feel good for your body.

Dance. Skip. Take a long nap. Pamper yourself from head to toes.

Dare to look at yourself in the mirror. And then do it again naked.

What does thinking about all of this body aware self-care feel like?

Don't Call It Dancing!

Another wonderful way to ground yourself and shake off the incessant mind chatter is to dance. But don't call it dancing.

Because that will immediately make you self-conscious, like you have to know the steps, and look good, and be graceful.

Call it 'moving your body to music' instead.

And get yourself some tulle. You know, that fine, netted material that ballerinas wear as a tutu. It's light, it's pretty and it's unpredictable.

It's how I learned to move in my own body.

A friend had long ago given me a book called Juggling for Dummies. It came with three small pieces of white tulle, each about six inches long. The book instructed me to toss them up and catch them. Unlike plastic balls or bowling pins, the tulle was light, and I could toss them high into the air and have plenty of time to position my hands and body to catch them before they hit the floor.

When I added music, my whole world changed. I wasn't dancing, I was moving my body with the music.

I'd toss a tulle scarf high above me, extending my arms out

through my fingertips to catch it. There was a lightness, a silliness in the movements that took away all self-consciousness.

I added my torso and legs into each stretch, reaching with my whole body. If I missed the scarf, I'd follow it toward the floor, bending and tucking, graceful as the scarves themselves floating in the air. Always, I was following the scarf, not leading with my body.

Different music inspired different movements. I moved with classical and jazz and African drumming. I especially loved the slower music because it made me more aware of every turn and stretch of my arms and legs and torso.

I played with stop motion, pausing with one foot up in the air, like I was in mid-step. Without even trying, I was building strength in my legs and improving my balance.

I added a second scarf, and tossed them each independently, moving my body left, then right to catch them both before they hit the floor. Sometimes I tossed them up together, rushing to catch both. Sometimes I let them intentionally float to the floor where I met them, my body curled like a ball, waiting.

I discovered that moving to a particular sad piece of music helped me grieve a recent breakup. My body could feel the sadness and the pain and the loss and release it without me getting caught up in the story of it all.

Moving to music became a daily ritual, an afternoon act of creative expression. It was a wonderful interlude between my work day and my personal life.

These days, I move in the morning, after the dog walking and before I sit down to write. Moving with music gets me out of my head and reconnects me with my breath, my body and my heart.

HEART SPARKS

Don't think—move your body!

I invite you to get yourself some tulle, put on some music and move your body, following the scarves.

And let me how you like it!

Wherever You Are Is Where You Begin

Wherever you are is where you begin. Right here. Right now. Never mind how you've tried it before, done it before, been there before.

You are here. Now. Standing in this present moment.

While this may be an easy concept to accept abstractly, it is not as easy to embrace when we are attempting to do something we used to be so good at.

I used to be a cyclist. I took daily rides of 10-15 miles along the canals, to city parks. I easily pedaled 35-50 miles every Saturday, touring the stretches of farmland on the outskirts of Phoenix. I even did a 2-day, 150 mile ride from Phoenix to Parker Dam on the California border as a fundraiser for MS.

When I think of those long rides, I forget that when I first started, it was a huge accomplishment to ride just one mile around my own neighborhood.

I forget that it took months for me to build up my physical and mental strength and endurance to ride long distances.

It's been more than 20 years since I was that long distance rider. In fact, my bike has been tucked into a corner, gathering cobwebs for the last year. But when I think about riding, I remember how free I can feel pedaling in the breeze, how strong my body can be, balanced and self-propelling me.

And I want to feel that again.

And I know I have to start where I am.

The keys to building strength and endurance with any new activity are consistency, frequency and increasing the level of activity each time.

It's also important to be patient, gentle and realistic with your progress. And it helps a lot to hold a vision of yourself already accomplishing what is it that you are just beginning.

I got my bike tuned up and steam cleaned. I bought a bike computer so I can see how many minutes and how many miles I ride each time. I am setting do-able goals, increasing the time and distance of my ride every couple of days.

And I'm holding a picture of myself, pedaling strong and easy over new terrain, confident in the saddle, smiling into the breeze.

 *HEART SPARKS*

What new activity or mindset are you working with?

Just begin where you are.

Begin with how you are.

Just begin.

How Yoga Works: A Personal Story

We all have bad days. You know, when everybody bugs you, when nothing anyone does is good enough, when you wish you could run away for a while, even from yourself.

In an ideal world we could retreat from the world and wait for the moodiness to pass. But in this real world, how do you find your way back to your own center?

I was dangerously grouchy with the world this morning. I was annoyed at the school boy riding his bike on the sidewalk instead of in the bike lane. I was curt with the woman at the grocery store for talking with the previous customer when it was clearly my turn. I grumbled at the way my neighbor parked beyond the lines, making it difficult for me to back out. I felt like I should have had yellow caution taped wrapped around me, as fair warning.

Usually, I am able to honor and accept the ways and rules that people choose for themselves without letting their behaviors annoy or aggravate me. But this morning for whatever strange reason (maybe hormones), I had no compassion, no patience, no benevolence. At all.

Fortunately, I have my weekly yoga practice. In the sacred

space of my yoga class, I stepped onto my mat and allowed myself to release whatever was harboring those uncompassionate feelings. It didn't need a name or a reason. It was just energy that wasn't serving me and I needed to let it go.

I breathed into my core, imagining only strength, no emotion at all. I followed my breath to the bottoms of my feet and felt the floor, the ground, the earth, supporting me as I let it all go. And then I breathed into my belly, my lungs and lifted my heart toward forgiveness and gratitude. I know it sounds hokey but this is what yoga is for me.

Yoga is more than the physical poses, the bending and stretching and strengthening of my outer body. Yoga is also connecting with my breath and stretching and strengthening my inner body. Yoga helps me integrate my physical energy with my spiritual energy. Yoga is how I connect my individual self with the greater life force that is each of us.

And when I am part of this connection, I no longer feel angry with the bike rider or impatient with the grocery clerk or frustrated with my neighbor's parking skills. Instead, I am able to lean back into compassion for each of them, and I can more easily, more freely, accept the choices they have made.

I started going to yoga classes nine years ago to become more flexible. Little did I know that the flexibility would translate beyond just how far I could bend to touch my toes.

I have become more flexible with how I approach my entire life, from letting go of strict schedules and deadlines and not wearing a watch, to sitting back and giving people the space they need to do their own growing.

Yoga introduced me to my spiritual essence and the deeper inner wisdom of my body. When I was recovering from open heart surgery several years ago, it was my yoga practice that helped me stay patient and present and focused on healing. Even before I could return to class, I would sit in my chair at home and just breathe, relaxing, releasing, healing.

My yoga practice reminds me that it doesn't matter if someone else can bend further or reach higher, that we each need to only focus on our own best selves and to tune in and listen to our own bodies as we stretch to our own soft edge.

And so, when I find myself comparing myself to someone, or judging someone for how they are acting, I come back to my yoga practice, to my breath, to my heart, back to that place where we say Namasté.

When I honor the light and love in me where the entire universe resides, and I honor the light and love in you where the entire universe resides, then there is only one of us.

 ***HEART SPARKS***

How do you find your way back to your center?

Practice 2:

Quieting

What Does Quiet Sound Like?

We say we want to know our heart's desire. We want to know what we love, what we should be doing with our lives. We want to know what really matters. But our lives are so full of television and traffic, and music in our ears and demands on our shoulders, that we can't hear our deepest thoughts and desires.

We are so used to believing the old tapes and the learned behaviors, that we don't know what is really true and authentic anymore.

And so the first step is to pay less attention to all of that noise in our lives and start listening to what else there might be.

I was invited to dinner at a friend of a friend's house. After hugs all around I was led into the combined kitchen-dining-living room area with Saltillo tile floors, granite counters, stainless appliances and a 42" television blaring CNN.

I was grateful when the hostess picked up the remote, but was surprised when she merely turned the volume down instead of turning it off completely.

Even when we sat down to the lovely meal she had

prepared and the three of us were engaged in joyous chatter, the TV was still humming in the background.

I meet a lot of people who keep the TV on when they're home alone. Or they've got the radio going, or their iPad shuffling. Even when they aren't in the same room as the noise, it is there, as background, so that they are never left in the quiet to hear their own mind chatter.

I get this.

But mind chatter is a lot like a three year old child tugging at the leg of your pants -- until you give them your attention and answer their questions, the tugging will persist.

If we don't deal with the chatter, the chatter will never stop.

And until we can listen beyond the chatter, we will never hear the deeper, quieter, stronger voice of our own heart.

This idea of getting quiet might scare the pants off of you. And maybe, at the same time, you're curious about this other voice that I'm talking about. Maybe you do want to hear the voice of your heart.

And so let this desire to know lead the way.

My favorite way to make any change is not to stop doing something, but to begin doing something else.

So, instead of forcing a mandatory NO TV moratorium, why not do something that will help you embrace the silence.

If I asked you, right now, to go sit quietly and meditate, chances are you'd sit there and your mind would quickly fill with a ticker tape of to do's and plans, what your best friend said on the phone last night, and where you wish you could go on vacation next year. You might hear your third grade teacher's voice berating you for daydreaming or your mother, reminding you to sit still, and then you might suddenly remember the thing you forgot to get at the grocery store. And the whole time you would be beating yourself up for having all of these thoughts when you were supposed to be blissfully meditating.

So I'm not going to ask you sit quietly. Not yet.

Instead I'm going to invite you to do something physical. Often, just moving in your body can shift the noise right out of your head.

 **HEART SPARKS**

Go for a walk.

Or take a shower.

Or play Frisbee with your dog.

Do something physical without a background soundtrack.

Pay attention to any thoughts or feelings that show up.

The Practice Of Noticing

Every morning after walking the dogs, I fill the birdfeeder and sit out on my back patio with my coffee and a bowl of bran cereal, no milk, sprinkled with dried cranberries and sometimes a half of a banana, sliced, and the birds and I have breakfast together.

This regular morning time is my opening time, my quieting time, my daily meditation. It is the space where I am not in my thoughts, my ideas, or my to-dos, but instead, I am focused on the world outside of me: the sky colors, the array of birds at the feeder, how the pecking order changes from sparrow to mourning dove to pigeon.

But for the past two weeks it has been too cold to sit outside in the mornings and instead, I've been having my coffee with my email. And today, it caught up with me.

My head was spinning with too many thoughts: preparations for tomorrow's workshop, remembering to treat the stain on my brown shirt before doing the laundry, the things I will teach a room full of salespeople about their new iPads, what I'm having for lunch, how to structure the next Mac training videos, and on and on and on. And I knew I needed to get out of my head or I would spin myself crazy.

I pulled on my sweatshirt and took my coffee outside. I filled the bird feeder and waited. The litany of thoughts raced in my head and there was no flurry of flapping at the feeder to distract me. There were no birds at all. I guess they come later when it is this chilly.

So I focused instead on listening.

I heard the cars on 7th Street, a trash truck raising and lowering several blocks away, a string of short, high pitched chirpings in the neighbor's tree. Then I caught a flash of movement in the mulberry tree. I scanned the bare gray branches and spotted a single towhee perched in stillness, his body puffed up against the cold. I kept my eyes on him but he wasn't moving, and soon the babble of thoughts started up again.

Several minutes passed before I realized I was thinking about work and no longer watching the bird.

I took a deep breath, consciously following it in and then out, slowly bringing my awareness out of my head and back into my body: me, sitting in my chair, in my yard, watching a towhee on a bright winter morning.

I scanned the tree again, looking for the bird. He had moved to a branch closer to the feeder, but he still wasn't moving much. It took so much concentration to stay with him.

I traced the outline of his body with my eyes, discerning the short beak, skinny legs, the flash of brown on his underbelly.

I tuned into a rustling and noticed a second towhee on the ground, pushing the mulch with his feet. His body looked browner in the light, his eye a beady red circle.

The bird in the tree jumped onto the feeder and poked his beak into the filled tube, then flung a beak full of seeds onto the ground. The bird on the ground scurried over and pecked them up.

I watched them for a while longer, then took my coffee inside to gather my calmer but still swirling thoughts, vowing to sit outside the next morning, and the next again, to begin the practice of quieting.

I don't often have this kind of mind chatter. And I'm sure it's because I have a regular practice of quieting. But, like any practice, if you don't do it for a while, even a little while, it loses its effect and it takes time to get back to it.

It's the same if you go to the gym regularly. Each time the workout gets easier as you build stamina, endurance. But if you take a month off, you may be surprised that you've lost some of your strength.

And so you begin again, where you are...without judgment... without impatience or frustration or beating yourself up...

You sit.

You breathe.

You notice.

This Practice of Noticing is about slowing down and being with what is present around you. Without judgment. It is about moving out of the mind and into the physical body where you can be present with where you are.

And yes, it is a practice. In the same way a musician practices scales or an athlete practices their sport, this Practice of Noticing, of paying attention, will be something you do regularly, with the intention of getting "better" at it.

Because the more you do it, the more you do it. Not just when you're sitting still, but when you're waiting in line at the supermarket, or having trouble falling asleep. Just zoom out of your head and notice where you are. And breathe.

And if those chattering voices want to join you, or you begin to berate yourself for sitting when you could be doing other, more important things, re-connect with your breath, and send those voices on their way, like clouds floating by in pretty blue sky.

 **HEART SPARKS**

Find something to watch. To observe.

Without judgment or thought.

Just detach and connect.

Keep coming back.

Chances are, you will probably enjoy it. And you might even feel calmer, less stressed, and more relaxed than you did before the practice.

Create your own Practice of Noticing.

Get a notebook or sketchbook and begin a Book of Observations to record what you experience.

Take photographs or collect things. Write or draw or sketch what you see.

This is not about writing about your feelings, although, if something comes up, certainly, follow it. This is about connecting with something beyond your own mind chatter, and creating a space of quiet for you to record, observe, step back and pay attention to what else, what all, there is.

You can use the practice of Quieting in all kinds of situations to relieve stress, regain focus and make heart-centered choices.

Un-Limiting Your Beliefs

When I was in my twenties I imagined that I would be the next Great American Writer. I sat at my portable electric Royal typewriter every day, inventing stories about people, documenting my observations, journaling ideas for my first great novel.

One afternoon a good friend said to me, "Why do you bother? There are no new ideas. Everything's already been said."

Now, she was an important person in my life, and very smart—- her IQ was high enough to join the Mensa Society —- and so I believed her.

And I stopped writing.

Twenty years later I took a deep breath and signed up for a creative writing class with an amazing teacher who encouraged my writing, challenged my skills and inspired me to write deeper and better.

One day she said, "There are no new ideas."

My heart sank to my knees. No, not again.

And then she finished her sentence.

"And so it's your job as a writer to come up with new

ways to say things so that people can see it fresh. New."

Her words gave me permission to pursue this thing that I love so much. More important, I believed in my writing again.

These kinds of limiting beliefs are part of the mind chatter that often holds us back from tapping into that wondrous place of passion and creation inside of us.

But when we sit down with them, really try them on, we can discern if they're true, if they still fit, or if, in fact, they're holding us back from the real truth.

 **_HEART SPARKS_**

Choose a belief that you currently have that you would like to change. Maybe it's the voice that talks you out of doing something you really want to try.

On a blank piece of paper, write the complete message.

Now ask yourself:

In what ways does this belief affect my life?

Who in my life supports this belief?

How does my role in my workplace/relationships support this belief?

Now think about a new, healthier message that you would like to have that would replace the old message. Write that new message on a clean piece of paper.

In what ways would this new message affect my life?

Who in my life would support this new message and how would they do that?

How would my work place/relationships support this new message?

How would my personal and professional life (including decisions) reflect this revised message?

What is the first step I will take to embrace this new message?

Life Is a Spiral, Not a Circle

Many of us believe we are here to learn lessons. And when those same lessons slam us over and over again, we think we have failed because we still are being offered the same lessons.

But we aren't walking the same ground. We are not retracing our steps. Yes, we are returning to these ideas, but we are seeing things from a different perspective.

Imagine you are driving up a mountain road. The road curves and turns so that you cannot always see where you've come from or where you're going. You pull off at a vista point and you can see the valley below you. Imagine that vast landscape is your life. To the left, and right, and far in the distance you can see the choices you've made and the people you've loved.

Drive a little further on the mountain road and pull off at another vista point, and the valley is wider, more colorful in the light, and you see other things you've done, different people who have impacted your life.

Further up the mountain you stop at another vista point. The things that seemed so difficult are much further away, part of the beautiful valley spread out before you. You can see a glimpse of the road you've been on and the road ahead, high and above you.

Each turn of the mountain road gives you a new perspective, a different way to see where you've been. Every curve offers you a chance to slow down and pay closer attention. And at the top of the mountain you are able to really see how far you've come.

Even driving back down the mountain on the same road is not going to be the same as driving up. The view will different. Driving on the inside lane may feel safer. And, having been to the top, you may notice new things at each vista point.

 ***HEART SPARKS***

When you think of your life like a drive up a mountain, what do you see?

What is the road like?

What kind of mountain is it?

What season is it?

Draw a map of your road up the mountain and mark the vista points.

What new perspectives do you have?

Seeing What Is Unseen

A thick layer of fog fills the folds in the hills behind me, like blankets rolled up at the door to keep out the draft. Morro Rock is gone from my view, though I know it is standing somewhere behind the stretch of gray that rises higher than the Los Osos hills.

Across the creek, the fog settles over the buildings on Ocean Avenue like the puffy white clouds you see out of an airplane window and I can barely make out the shops and the cars parked on the street. Sounds are louder, while, at the same time, everything seems more still.

I remember a time in my life when I felt like my whole world was engulfed in this kind of thick unseeing fog. It was unsettling, disorienting, anxiety producing. Because I was trying to move through it.

I was desperately wanting to not to be in the uncomfortableness that I was feeling, the sense of being lost, the place of not knowing. But the more I tried to push through, the harder it was to see.

Until I stopped trying and was able to be with the discomfort, sit with the feeling of not knowing, relax my whole being into the gray that was all around me.

We've all experienced a time in our lives when we have felt lost. Undirected. Uncomfortable not knowing what's next.

Our tendency is to run, make a plan, rush toward something, anything that is more comfortable than sitting still. But often, staying, sitting, being with the not knowing is the only way to discover what's next.

These days I love the fog because it is a visual call to be still. The fog reminds me that this is not a time to navigate a new path, but to look inside, to see the things that are unseen.

One of my favorite children's books, which I didn't read until I was an adult, is Madeleine L'Engle's A Wrinkle In Time. It is a story of time travel and good versus evil and it is filled with wisdom and life lessons. One of the themes is to look for the unseen, like music, joy, and love.

These same wise words come from Antoine de Saint Exupéry's The Little Prince, when he tells his friend, "One sees clearly only with the heart. What is essential is invisible to the eye."

When we are in this hazy, foggy space of not seeing our paths clearly, we tend to panic. We think we are lost because we cannot see our way through.

But if we allow ourselves to relax into the stillness, it

becomes a gift, a quieting where we can hear our heart beat, where we can turn our attention to the things unseen.

By sitting still, looking and listening inward, we may realize we aren't lost at all. In this quiet haze of seeing the unseen, we are, in fact, just coming home.

HEART SPARKS

How do you see the unseen?

How do you find ways to be with the fog?

Practice 3:

Exploring

Love the Questions

"Be patient toward all that is unsolved in your heart and try to love the questions themselves, like locked rooms and like books that are now written in a very foreign tongue. Do not now seek the answers, which cannot be given you because you would not be able to live them. And the point is, to live everything. Live the questions now. Perhaps you will then gradually, without noticing it, live along some distant day into the answer."

~ Rainer Maria Rilke

I have seen it happen with so many of my clients. As they begin to open up to their own quiet and create some space, they feel lighter. They feel hopeful. They are willing to try something new.

Instead of staying stuck in their old responses, they are ready to explore what else they might want in life.

Exploring isn't about finding new answers. It's about asking new questions.

Growing up, we are trained to seek the answers. To know how things work. To learn how to control ourselves and our lives.

As I've gotten older I have come to understand Rilke's

words, that the questions themselves are the stepping stones toward our heart's desire. That each new question, posed with curiosity and inquisitiveness, opens us up to something we may not have considered or imagined before.

Have you ever watched toddlers? They grab at eye-catching objects, reach for new surfaces, toddle beyond their familiar terrain. They are curious about everything.

As we open to our own hearts, we too become curious. We notice more, we feel braver, we begin to consider things from a new perspective. It's as if we are exploring our world for the first time. And we begin to feel safe enough to ask ourselves deeper questions.

But I promise you, if you haven't laid the groundwork first with your quieting and grounding, you're probably going to come up with the same answers that you always have.

Exploring can be fun. It takes us out of our daily routine. It challenges us with new possibilities and choices. Many of my clients report that, when I ask them to Go Exploring, it brings more fun and surprise into their lives than they've experienced in years.

One woman said that she would have never taken herself to an ethnic market, but she had so much fun looking at all of the foreign labels, and the colorful produce. She even bought some vegetables she had never eaten before and loved looking up recipes online. It reminded her how much she loved to cook new foods.

As we give ourselves permission to explore and discover new experiences, something happens. We remember things we used to love. We remember things we used to dream about. We feel a lightness, an energy stirring inside of us.

Really.

It's the spark. It's remembering that we do feel passionate about something. It's reconnecting with our deepest visions and dreams for ourselves. It is knowing that there really is something we want to be and do with our lives.

This is that thing called passion.

And passion is what fuels us. What gives us our juice. It's that feeling that you get when you're so engaged in something that you could do this thing all day, all night, even if you weren't being paid.

The more you explore and experiment and follow your own questions and curiosities, the more you will discover what this might be for you, what you are truly passionate about and what you might really want to be doing with your life.

 *HEART SPARKS*

What have you always dreamed of ?

What are you curious about?

Where might another road lead?

How would you feel if you took that risk?

What did you want to be when you were six years old?

What's your favorite way to play?

What makes you smile?

Where can you go exploring in your own home town?

List some of your favorite things to do and what, specifically about them do you most enjoy.

Look over your list and notice similarities. Notice differences.

Boasting and Bragging

As a kid, Peter Pan was my favorite fictional character. Not because he never grew up, but because he was so cocky and confident. And he could fly. I had the record album from the Broadway play with Mary Martin and I sang it over and over.

My favorite song was "I've Gotta Crow" and I sang it every day, all day for months. I'm sure it contributed to my own self-confidence, singing:

"Conceited? Not me,
It's just that I am what I am
And I'm me!
When I look at myself
And I see in myself
All the wonderful things that I see
If I'm pleased with myself
I have every good reason to be."

For my 6th birthday, my mother took me and my best friend Ellen to see the live play. We had seats all the way up in the balcony, far from the stage, but so high up that I could see the wires that Peter Pan flew on. It was wondrous, seeing him fly right by us, singing, so full of himself.

But most of us are taught not to brag about ourselves. That it's impolite to draw attention to ourselves. In fact, many of us don't even know how to accept praise for the things we do.

But it's so important to acknowledge our accomplishments, to honor our gifts and talents, to celebrate the feel-good moments of our lives.

 *HEART SPARKS*

What are you good at?

What do people come to you for?

What are you proud of about yourself?

Make a list of everything you've done this year, last year, your whole life if you want. Big things, little things...take your time to really remember.

Now pick a few from your list and **shout them, out loud,** with pride!

Pat yourself on the back for a job well done!

Often, when we acknowledge and accept what we have accomplished, it gives us the confidence to try something new.

What new thing would you like to see on the list that you'd like to accomplish in the next few months?

Breaking the Rules: The Joys of Spontaneity

We all have rules that we live by. I'm not talking about the rules of etiquette or morals. I'm talking about the mind-messing rules we've created for ourselves that often keep us pigeon-holed in our old habits and limiting ways of thinking.

I'm talking about the rules we've talked ourselves into like, "I can only work with clients if I charge an hourly rate." Or, "I can only sign up for a class for myself AFTER the kids are all in school." Or, "I have to exercise every day of the week, otherwise I've failed."

Rules are great for giving us structure. But rules can often keep us from branching out, expanding our thinking and living bigger.

Last weekend I broke all the rules.

I didn't wake to an alarm. I didn't take a shower first thing. In fact, I stayed in my pajamas for two hours before officially starting my day.

By NOT doing things the way I ALWAYS do them, the whole weekend opened up for me. I rode my bike. I spent a good chunk of the day writing and I even enjoyed some time in my yard, pulling the cat claw that is choking the back fence.

And on Sunday, instead of helping a friend do some stuff around her house, we took the dogs to the river and had a picnic. It was spontaneous. It was unplanned. And it was wonderful. We even stopped at a small farmer's market on the way home (one of my favorite things to do.)

Sure, discipline and structure are important. They are the reasons my businesses run so smoothly and effortlessly.

But I'm finding that a balance of structure and spontaneity best supports me, both in my work life AND in my personal life.

I used to have a rule that I said NO to anything not pre-planned or on the schedule. This kept me organized and in control.

But by saying YES to booking a last minute client, suddenly, there were more opportunities in my working day. Saying YES to a friend's impromptu invitation meant more FUN! By being open and flexible and saying YES to spontaneity, all kinds of things are opening up in my life.

Changing the rules means doing things differently. Doing things differently creates different outcomes.

But before we can consciously choose a new way, we have to first notice what rules we have created that may seem to be working for us, but are actually keeping us stuck.

My old rule was to just keep doing what I'm doing, because it worked.

My new approach is to PAUSE at each opportunity, and ask myself, How do I really feel about this? What if I did this a different way?

 *HEART SPARKS*

What rules have you created for your life?

Which ones are working?

Which ones are actually holding you back more than they are supporting you?

How can you start breaking your own rules?

How might your life change if you did?

Why is How

I had lunch last week with a woman who I haven't seen in almost six years. In all of our catching up, I told her about my open heart surgery, the growth of Spark the Heart, the new Mac training videos, and she was in awe of how much I have bloomed.

"It's because I quit smoking pot," I told her.

She knew I had smoked and she was curious why I chose to quit.

"Because it was the one thing keeping me from what I really wanted."

I loved being stoned. I was highly creative, very functional (I didn't smoke until after my working day), and it was a wonderful escape from the depression of a recent break up. When I was high I felt so connected to something bigger in myself.

And that became the problem.

What I wanted more than anything was to feel connected to others, to feel connected to something bigger than myself.

But, being stoned all the time, I was usually too spacey to drive or too tired to go out, too fixated on feeling good to risk any vulnerability.

And then, there was that day, that moment, that I realized I couldn't have what I truly wanted if I continued to get high.

And so I quit. Cold turkey. Just like that.

Sure, the first few months were challenging and uncomfortable. But each time I thought about getting high, I immediately reminded myself that it was ultimately not what I wanted. And, instead, I'd call a friend, get out of my house, make a connection.

It wasn't enough to just not smoke. It was equally important for me to replace the behavior with what I really wanted. I needed to focus on the big WHY of what I was doing.

Our why grounds us in the deepest truth of who we are. It's the reason it feels so good when we're doing it. There is no struggle. The path is clear. We may not know what or when or how, but our Why is how our heart leads the way.

Sometimes, though, we are so lost, we don't know our why. We have no clue about anything, really.

And that's OK.

Instead of thinking about your why, focus on how you want to feel.

I wanted to feel connected to something bigger than myself. I wanted to feel like my work mattered. That I mattered. I wanted to feel more alive. That became my why.

Once you connect with your Why, everything else will open up.

Because your Why fuels your intentions and your actions. Your Why helps you through when it's really uncomfortable. Your why can save you from that chocolate chip cookie. Your why can get you walking at six in the morning. Your Why will have your back when you step up onto the big stage.

Your why is your super power. Your magic elixir. Your Why is how you move through any transformation.

 *HEART SPARKS*

What it is that you really want for yourself?

Why do you want it?

How will you feel doing it?

Is there one thing keeps you from being or doing or feeling this?

What would it take to make the commitment to this real desire?

How can you begin to replace the thing that holds you back with the thing you truly want?

Inspiration From the Keyboard

There are clues to our happiness all around us and the secret to discovering them is to simply pay attention. To slow down enough to notice the details around us. To be still long enough to hear the quieter, stronger voice inside.

Often, we are so distracted by the noise and activity of our daily lives that we are oblivious to the beauty, the wisdom, and the inspiration of what is right in front of us.

The other day I saw an image online of a PC keyboard with the Control, Alt and Delete Keys highlighted, and I immediately thought, WOW, Great questions!

What am I trying to CONTROL?

What do I need to ALTER in my life?

What am I ready to DELETE?

Inspiration is everywhere, all around us. Too often, we just aren't paying attention and so life goes on, same as it ever was. And we go on, stuck in the patterns of our days, far removed from what we might really want to be doing.

But when we pause and ask ourselves these kinds of hard questions, we are honoring that deep desire inside us for something better, more exciting, more joy-full.

By simply recognizing what isn't working in our lives, we

open up to the possibility of creating more of what IS working. But we have to be willing to ask.

 *HEART SPARKS*

I invite you to find a quiet place with a blank piece of paper and ask yourself these powerful questions:

What are you trying to Control in your life?

How might things be different if you let go of that control?

What do you need to Alter in your life?

If you changed just one thing, what would that open up for you?

What are you ready to Delete?

What thought or relationship or activity or habit does not support who you are and the work you want to do in this world?

Remember the Magic Eight Ball?

One of my favorite toys as a kid was the Magic Eight Ball. It was a black plastic about the size of my opened hand, that looked like an eight ball pool cue. You asked it a YES or NO question, gave it a good shake while you concentrated on the question and an answer magically appeared in the glass window on the bottom.

Sometimes the answer was Yes, Definitely. Sometimes it said My Sources Say No. Sometimes it answered Ask Again Later. Of course, I always re-asked and re-shook the ball until I got the answer I wanted.

As adults, we use many kinds of oracle-like tools for guidance. We throw the I-Ching coins, pick Runes, read our horoscopes and Tarot cards.

We are looking for answers, confirmation, proof that we are on the right path. And yet, often when we get an answer, we keep asking again, just to be sure.

In a recent Living Room Ladies, we were using a deck of oracle cards to tap into our subconscious insights. One woman chose a card and laughed out loud.

"This is just so perfect," she said. It was an image of a

spirit woman looking over a human woman. "This is exactly what I've been saying-I need to trust the higher wisdom that is in me."

And then she asked if she could pick another card.

This time I laughed. I suggested that, no matter how many cards she picked, the same message would appear. Because that's the answer she is needing to hear right now. I asked her if she still wanted to pick another card. She did. And it was, of course, a very similar image.

Another woman in the group also completely connected with the image on her first card. She too, drew a second card and the image and the message were almost identical to her first card.

How many times do you need to hear the answer before you believe it, trust it, know it to be true?

 ***HEART SPARKS***

What question are you asking, over and over, because you want a different answer?

What might happen if you accepted the answer you keep getting?

What I Learned From Making Blueberry Pancakes

As a kid I often ate waffles and ice cream for breakfast. Or a bowl of Lucky Charms without the milk. Or Sugar Pops, without a spoon, one sweet, sticky kernel at a time.

On weekends we'd have bagels and lox and whitefish from the deli. Sometimes my father made scrambled eggs with thick round slices of Hebrew National salami, or French toast with Log Cabin syrup.

But I don't remember ever having homemade pancakes. The only time I remember eating them was on those rare occasion that the family would go to IHOP for breakfast and I would order a plate full of silver dollars with no butter. I'd drown them in the thick brown maple syrup from the fancy pitcher with the sticky metal spout.

My first attempt at making pancakes from scratch was for my friend's twentieth birthday. I mixed the flour and milk according to the recipe and poured the batter into the frying pan. I didn't know that the pan needed to be hot before you started, or that you shouldn't flip them more than once on each side.

My dream birthday breakfast turned into a batter-y burned mess, the apartment filled with smoke and my friend laughed at my lack of pancake making skills.

That was thirty five years ago and, while I love to eat pancakes, in all those years I have never tried to make them again.

But several weeks ago I bought a box of Bisquick instant, just-add-water pancake mix and a bottle of real maple syrup from Canada. I had an inkling that I wanted to try again but, since both items have a long shelf life, I wasn't under any pressure to make them right away.

But last night I had a craving. So I pulled out the box, measured out the mix, added the water and whisked it together. I coated the frying pan with non-stick spray like the directions said, put the flame on medium heat and let the pan get hot.

Then I poured a four inch blob of batter into the pan and dotted the pancake with some fresh blueberries.

And I watched the clock, waiting.

The directions on the box said to flip it after a minute or a minute and a half, or when the edges started to brown.

I guess my pan wasn't hot enough because when I peeked my spatula under the pancake to check, the bottom was still white and sticky.

So I waited some more.

As I stood there, watching the blobs of batter in the pan, I realized that this is why I don't like cooking. Because it is a lot of waiting. And not a lot of doing.

They say that, how we do one thing is how we do everything. As I stood over the hot pan, watching for the edges to brown, it became very clear to me that I am a do-er, not a wait-er. I'm a person of action, of results, of energy in motion.

This doesn't mean that I can't sit still. Because if sitting still is the thing that I am doing, then I'm fine with it.

But when I think about how I step into any new habit, or begin a new project, I see how much I don't like to just wait.

Even though I know that life is a flow of action and non-action, and that there needs to be space in between, I am always doing something else while I am waiting, keeping busy, stirring another pot of possibility. I am never just doing nothing, waiting for the next step.

And it occurs to me that maybe I wouldn't feel so scattered and unfocused if I leaned into this waiting space and didn't try to fill up every minute with doing something, or doing something else.

Waiting is about giving up the need for control. It is

allowing something to happen in its own time, giving a thing or a person the space to bloom, ready, or, in the case of a pancake, time to brown.

I guess I need to make pancakes more often so that I can practice waiting for things to happen in their own time.

Without control. Without impatience. Without doing anything else.

As for my first batch of blueberry pancakes, I won't lie and tell you that they were the best pancakes I've ever had. But they weren't the worst either. I drowned them in the maple syrup from Canada and was pretty proud of myself for sticking with it. And especially proud for seeing how this simple act of making pancakes could teach me something about how I do everything else in my life.

 *HEART SPARKS*

What does this story spark about how you do things?

Practice 4:

Getting Clear

The Energy of Intention

As you begin to explore what you love, something happens. You remember a dream you once had. You get excited about some project or you remember something someone told you about your greatness. You realize that you do feel passion and that you could actually change your life and live your dreams.

At first, it may be a whole scene in your mind, or a full-body sensation of excitement. Or maybe you've written pages and pages about it all in your journal.

Suddenly, you're seeing the possibility of a new horizon for yourself. Maybe it is a new way of being in your body. Or a new kind of work. Maybe you are opening up to more vulnerability.

By honing this thing to a single I AM intention, you are able discern what, about this vision, is calling you. By setting an intention, you create clarity for yourself. By forming a single sentence, clearly stating what you want, you are announcing to the Universe that you are ready.

I am a best-selling author who leads amazing retreats and is an inspiring, sought-after speaker.

I choose healthy foods for my body.

I like to move in my body with joy and ease in different ways and at different times of the day.

I have the strength and stamina and everything I need to do this.

I use my voice to express who I really am.

Intentions are always written in the present tense, as if you are already doing/being/having it.

I've heard people say that intention is thoughts with legs. That it isn't enough to just want something - you have to take some kind of action toward this thing you desire..

Setting an intention gives you direction. It is a point on your heart's compass. It is an affirmation of what you want to manifest for yourself.

From the Latin intentio(n), intention means, "stretching, purpose."

I love that. Intention helps you grow towards your dreams.

As you get more in touch with your intentions, it's important to align what you want with how you live.

You can't be more authentic if you are working in a place that makes you feel the need to lie.

You can't be more creative if you hate the white walls of your room and avoid even thinking about changing them.

You can't be a millionaire if you are afraid to look into investing your money.

Being aware of these incongruities gives you a wonderful opportunity to make changes, to shift more toward how you truly want to show up in your life.

And knowing, clearly, what you want, makes it easier for you to find it.

During a Living Room Ladies gathering, we were talking about the energy of intention, and one of the women, Claire, shared that every day, for the past month, she has been reciting the intention, 'I want to take a tai chi class."

She had considered a place 45 minutes from her house and had even driven there on a Sunday to see how long it would take without traffic, but she realized it was too far and the wrong time of day.

So she let it go.

She looked online, googling tai chi in her neighborhood, but found nothing.

Again, she let it go.

Then, yesterday, she was at her doctor's office, waiting to pick up a prescription, and she saw a flyer on the counter offering free tai chi lessons in the same medical building. And it was less than 6 minutes from her house.

This is how intention works.

Ask and let go. Act and step back. Engage and surrender. Over and over again.

Claire took action steps toward her goal. And after each step, she let go. She didn't give up or stop trying. She just repeated her intention and let go of the outcome.

And she was paying attention.

Claire could have been so focused on getting her prescription and worrying about where she needed to be next and what should she make for dinner that she didn't notice the flyer.

But she was present, aware, and paying attention.

And she loves her new tai chi class.

 ***HEART SPARKS***

Do some free-writing about what you love and what you want and what you are wanting to manifest or become.

Free writing isn't about sentence structure or grammar or punctuation, or even making sense. It is following your pen on the paper, just writing freely, whatever comes up. Just start by writing the words I love...... and see where the writing takes you.. If you get stuck, come back to I love, or I want... and keep writing. you might want to set a time for 5 minutes and only write for that amount of time.

Then go back and hone it down to a single I AM statement of intention.

How can you continue to give this intention your attention?

What one single step can you take in the direction of your intention?

And how can you practice letting go of the outcome?

Waiting for Perfect….

When it comes to doing big heart stuff, our tendency is toward all or nothing. We want to wait for that perfect opportunity to begin living into our true self.

This is especially true with creative expression. We tell ourselves we need a designated space, a big chunk of scheduled time and all of the materials at hand before we can begin.

Unfortunately, this isn't how life happens.

And so we have to improvise the space, embrace the tiny pockets of time, and incorporate our creativity into our daily living.

Or we may be waiting forever.

Several years ago I discovered the joys of paper maché. I loved the freedom and simpleness of the materials: recycled newspaper and sticky, white glue that I shaped into bowls and clocks and found object sculptures.

I absolutely loved the organic process, how easy it was to wash the glue off my hands, how the pieces dried quickly in the desert heat. I worked outside on a thrift store wicker table on my back patio, close enough to the kitchen sink, and still, I could be as messy as I wanted to be.

When I moved to my current home three years ago, priorities shifted, I no longer had the wicker table and I stopped making art. But lately, I've been imagining my hands in the gluey gooiness again. I've been envisioning hearts of many sizes, all smaller than my palm, free-formed by my hands and then strung with beads and other found items.

But every time I thought about starting, I heard the voices in my head, "I have no room to work. With all of my business things, I have no time. With all of the creative energy I put into my businesses, I have no creativity left."

A few weeks ago I gave my Living Room Ladies a hugely creative assignment: To create a self-portrait expressing all that they had discovered about themselves in our work together.

As I described the project to them, I heard my own creative self speaking loudly, that all of this writing and business creating is one thing, but I wanted to start making things again.

Over the next few days I considered how I could make space for this kind of creative expression, both literally and figuratively.

Did I want to cut back on how often I write the Heart Sparks blog? Should I rearrange my office to create more work space? Should I just put it off like I have been for the last three years?

I asked the questions and waited for some definitive answers.

And then, one Saturday morning, I did it. I cleared the small counter next to my kitchen sink and put on my paint-smeared smock. I found an old metal roasting pan among my art supplies and poured in some glue, mixed in some water to thin it out and started tearing strips of newspaper that I had been saving for months.

I dipped the strips into the wet glue, pushing them under so they were completely coated. Then I slid the paper between my fingers to wipe off the excess glue. It was delicious.

I draped the wet strips over two small crumpled balls of newspaper, wrapping them together, then added more strips to shape them into a heart. I kept dipping and sliding and draping until it looked like a heart from all angles.

I made three hearts that first day, all different sizes and shapes, all smaller than my palm. They were jagged and awkward, different than I'd been imagining them, but in many ways, they looked even better than the pristine and perfect hearts I'd envisioned.

And I couldn't wait to try a new technique the next day.

The perfect time/space/lifestyle/net worth never comes. If you want something, you have to step away from the excuses and reconnect with the deeper passion, the drive, the inspiration for what you are dreaming. And then, just begin.

HEART SPARKS

What excuses are holding you back?

How can you let go of those voices and reconnect with the energy of your true passion?

The Power of a Word

Every year I choose a single word as a compass, a guide, a solid reminder of what I want to manifest for myself. The word serves as a touchstone for me as I make choices through the year. I post the word in my bathroom and acknowledge it daily, asking myself "how can I be that today?"

The first year I chose the word BE. Because I was always planning, dreaming and imagining the future, I was rarely present where I was.

BE-ing was very uncomfortable.

It made me slow down and experience where I was, not where I wanted to be NEXT. It made me sit still and feel my emotions. I began a yoga practice and discovered that the simple act of breathing can calm me and bring me back to the here and now.

The next year my word was VULNERABILITY. I wanted to let go of control and open to things that I didn't have the answers to. I was ready to feel what was uncomfortable and go even deeper.

I had so many opportunities during that year to practice this: with relationships, how I traveled, choosing to apply for a job that I didn't get. And I had emergency open heart surgery. Talk about vulnerability and letting go of control. It was the most amazing gift of an experience to be in that space of pure vulnerability and realize how much I was loved and supported.

The following year I chose ASK as a reminder that, even though I had fully recovered, I didn't have to do everything all by myself. I learned to ask for support, money, ideas, companionship.

More important, I learned that it's not about having the answers but being able to ask bigger questions and opening to the silence that is larger than me for deep and true inspiration.

Last year my word was INTEGRAYTION, intentionally spelled with the word gray in it because I wanted to let go of my extreme black and white thinking and live more in the grays. And I wanted to find ways to meld my two seemingly opposite work worlds together more, to let go of my all-or-nothing way of being.

A friend gifted me a beautiful necklace with the word stamped in silver and it was a lovely expression of further integrating my work with my personal life.

This year my word is EXPANSION. I want more space in my life. I want to show up bigger, both inside of myself and how I connect in the world. I want to open myself beyond what I already know and do well, to what else might be possible.

Expansion is all about breathing deeper and living at the edge of what is familiar and comfortable. And moving into that opened space with courage and intention and faith.

Already this year I have had several opportunities to do things that bring me right to that edge. And, scary as each activity has been, when I come back to my word, I see how saying YES completely supports my desire for expansion.

In the midst of all of this external expansion, it's just as important for me to also lean into the inner expansions I am creating - to breathe, and rest and be still and feel safe in this new and wondrous and sometimes vulnerable space.

 *HEART SPARKS*

What's your word for this year? You may come up with several. Take some time to discern the one that will best help you do and be this thing you are wanting.

Consider choosing a word that makes you uncomfortable, that will most clearly align you with who and what you are wanting to become.

How can using this word help you live a life you love?

Creating a Habitual Ritual

We all have something we love to do. But for whatever reason, we don't make the time. Other things seem more important. We neglect to schedule it in. We put it off until someday.

But if we want to do this thing that fills our heart, we can't wait. We have to make the time. It has to be a habit, a routine, a regular part of our daily life.

Routines become mundane. Often, the word habit has a negative connotation. We tend to break habits, think of bad habits. So why not, instead, create a habitual ritual.

A ritual is sacred. Important. Meaningful.

Like walking the dogs. Feeding the birds. Drinking your morning cup of coffee. An habitual ritual happens at a set time every day. Not every other day. Or once a week. But every day. Even if something else seems more important.

Nothing is more important.

You've learned this by NOT showing up. By talking yourself into other things, out of THIS thing. But then, you feel a hole in your heart, and food can't fill it. Sleep can't fill it. Not even dog kisses can fill it.

Only doing what you truly love can fill it.

It could be painting. Or exercising. Or learning a new language. It could be cooking or taking photographs or whatever you do that you can get lost in and when you look up at the clock three hours have passed.

For me, it is writing. How words miraculously appear on blank paper, flowing out from the end of my hand as if by magic. Sometimes they are boring, simple, repeating rhymes that any five year old could write.

But when I stay with it, a sentence forms, an image appears and a story unfolds like a fancy napkin in my lap and I just watch it, breathe it, follow it. Without censoring, without spell check, just allowing the words to lead and flow and color the page and I realize that it's not a hole in my heart at all, but a filling, an overfilling, an overflowing and THIS is what I have been missing. This is what I have been aching for. THIS is why I write.

And so, even on the days when all I can write are silly rhymes and simple descriptions of tall trees and a sky that is only blue, I must make it a habitual ritual to show up.

Because I want to write.

How do you create a habitual ritual?

You show up. At the same time everyday. Every Day. And you remember how much you want it. You come back to the WHY of doing this thing in the first place.

You honor the time, you honor yourself. You honor this thing you are setting out to do.

You pick up your paint brush, or put on your running shoes, or poise your finger pads over the grooves of the keyboard and you begin.

And the next day you begin again.

Create the ritual.Become the ritual.Because it's the only way to your heart.

 *HEART SPARKS*

What is that thing you love to do?

How can you begin to honor it and give it the space it needs?

The Story of Our Stories

Most of us love stories - the telling of a person's life, the happenings in a dream, great descriptions of people we've met and places we've been.

We also tell ourselves stories about what we can and cannot do and be and have. And often, we begin to believe that the stories we know and tell ourselves are the only truths.

We convince ourselves that, because, in the past, when we did this, the result was that, therefore, it will always be that way.

That because the last time you went to a party where you didn't know anyone, you were ignored and uncomfortable, now anytime you go somewhere where you don't know anyone, the same thing will happen.

Or that because every time you've submitted a piece of writing, it was rejected, so you'll never submit anything again for fear of another rejection.

We all have these repeating stories. And, because they are based in truth, we believe them. We hold them up and say, see, I'm not making this up. When I did that, this happened.

But, if we are truly writing our own life stories, then isn't it possible to write a new ending, even a brand new story?

I have worn eyeglasses since I was four years old and I have a lot of stories about how getting new glasses is hard, traumatic and always difficult.

There's the story about the octagonal tortoise shells in fifth grade that had such an improved prescription that I was nauseous for days.

Or the wire framed aviator glasses in high school that were too snug behind my ears, so I bent them and re-bent them until the metal temple broke, but I still wore them, even though they created an open sore on the side of my head.

Or, more recently, the very expensive, digitally-made lenses that I had to tilt my head to the left to find the sweet spot and I had them re-made and they still weren't right but they wouldn't give me a full refund.

In fact, in the last three years, I have paid for two different pairs of glasses that have ended up in the bottom of my drawer. So, even though I strain to read 12 point type, and my lenses are scratched and foggy, I'd rather wear a pair that has a five year old prescription than go through the whole New Glasses thing.

And, while, on some level I knew that this was a story that I didn't have to keep repeating, it wasn't until a friend said, "But it's just a STORY!!"

Until she pointed it out, I knew it but I didn't KNOW it. Or realize that I could write a NEW one.

So while I was in Phoenix, Marika made an appointment to get her eyes examined for a new prescription, and I made one too. And the exam was easy. And then we went shopping together for frames.

We looked in several stores and we both found some we liked at an independent optician in the neighborhood, an older man who really knows about glasses and fitting. I took a deep breath and ordered the frames and he said they'd be ready in a week.

But they weren't. And then it was Thanksgiving and the store was closed for the holiday weekend and I had to extend my stay in Arizona another week to wait for them.

I could feel my anxiety building and I noticed that I was beginning to sabotage the situation with my thoughts. "They're not going to be here in time." "I'm not going to like them." "This is going to be like all the other times."

I worked myself into quite a tizzy - should I cancel the order and just stick with what I have. After all, there was probably going to be something wrong with them.

And this is where the story changed.

Because I heard myself telling the old story. And I realized that I really WANTED these new glasses. I wanted to see better.

So I told myself that it might take some time to get used to the new prescription, but that it would be worth it if I could see clearer.

I took out a big piece of paper and wrote:

I will adjust to these wonderful glasses with patience and willingness, grace and ease. I will be so appreciative of the better vision.They're going to feel good and fit right.I'm going to love seeing myself in the mirror wearing them.

Folks will notice and like them.And my neck and shoulder pain will be gone.

I read and re-read these words all weekend, envisioning myself trying the new glasses on in the store and being happy.

The day I picked them up, I closed my eyes before I put the new glasses on and repeated that first line of my mantra, to remind myself to be patient and willing to get used to them.

With a few tweaks behind the ear and on the nose pieces, they were wonderful. I could read the smallest print on the bifocal card and the details on the sign across the street. And I didn't have a fish-bowl effect when I glanced sideways. The fact that he took $50.00 off the bill for the delays didn't hurt either.

It was amazing. Marika and I went to the grocery store and I was reading everything out loud, from the big signs at the far end of the aisles to the fine print on the cereal box. No squinting, no straining, no tilting my head every which way to find the sweet spot. I couldn't believe how easy it was!

The first time I saw myself in the bathroom mirror, I did a double-take. With a big grin. Yes, they're big and bold and fashion forward, but not eccentric. And I love having so much lens depth to see near, far and everything in between.

The next morning, Marika and I were sitting outside having our coffee and she said, "I still can't believe how easily you've adjusted to your glasses."

"I know," I said. "It really is all about the story we tell ourselves."

But there was a red tenderness on the left side of my nose and the back of the right earpiece was pressing too hard on the top of my ear.

The optician was closed for the weekend so I postponed my departure, scheduled two clients and went back to see him on Monday.

I was surprised that he called me by my name. I sat down and explained what hurt and he made some adjustments. The nose piece immediately felt better and the pressure on my ear was gone.

But after I got home I felt a new pressure along the side of my temple. And I started crying. Bawling. Because it was no longer easy. Because I hated this part about too tight, too loose.

Marika encouraged me to go back for another adjustment. She reminded me that they're just adjustments. That I already know that I can see with them, now it's about getting more comfortable. I cried some more, then asked her to go back with me. She even drove.

Sherwin, the optician, was just as happy to see me as the first time. He adjusted the right ear- piece so it was no longer pressing, tweaked the nose piece to re-center the frame and we left.

Marika asked, "Are you sure you don't want to walk around and try this for a while?"

"No, it's good. Let's just go home." But as we walked to the car, I wasn't sure.

"Can we just sit in the car for a minute?" We did, and after some more crying, I went back.

Sherwin and I played several rounds of too-tight-too-loose, and when I started to get frustrated, he said, "Just relax. Take your time." And in between each adjustment, he shared a story about his son, or the house he is building or he asked me a question about my Mac training.

And then I couldn't tell anymore how the fit was, so we

stopped. I thanked Sherwin and joined Marika who was waiting in the car.

By the evening I realized that, with all of the tweaking, the glasses were slightly crooked and the prescription was no longer in the right place.

But instead of freaking out and crying, I reminded myself that they were perfect before and they could be perfect again. That it wasn't a problem with the lenses, I just needed to get things adjusted again. And hey, maybe now that I had sharper distance vision, I'd start seeing what I want for my future.

So I chose to delay my departure back to California one more day, and I saw Sherwin again in the morning. He tweaked, he bent, he told me he's adjusted more than 10,000 glasses since he's been in business, and that sometimes, you have to go through Texas to get to Florida.

I laughed at the metaphor and thanked him for his patience.

My glasses are now pretty close to perfect. And I love seeing so much better. When my eyes are tired from the day, I remember that this is a transition, a process. That I just need to keep breathing and moving through.

And I'm still saying my affirmations, but this time, they're in the present tense.

I am adjusting to these wonderful glasses with patience

and willingness, grace and ease. I am so appreciative of the better vision.They feel good and fit right.I love seeing myself in the mirror wearing them. Folks notice and like them.My neck and shoulder pain is gone.

 *HEART SPARKS*

What stories do you keep repeating, reliving?

What if you re-wrote one?

How would this new story be different?

This. Here. Now.

This past holiday weekend Marika and I took the motorhome and the dogs to southeastern Arizona to see the migrating sandhill cranes. We camped at the Whitewater Draw Wildlife Refuge in the middle of desert brush, agricultural fields and man-made ponds created to attract migrating birds.

The refuge is surrounded by the Dragoon Mountains to the west and the Chiricahuas to the east, with Mexico just a short 25 miles to the south. And all around, a big wide sky of blue and birds.

We walked along the berms of the ponds as the sun set, the sky darkening against the crescendo of thousands of red winged blackbirds roosting in the reeds. Marika, an avid birder, pointed out a Harris Hawk circling above the field.

She counted unnamed sparrows flitting in the brush and we heard a Great Horned Owl in the nearby trees. A sky full of sandhill cranes circled the farthest ponds, grawking and honking as if they were conversing, where do you want to land?

Later, back in the RV, after dinner, my mind began to wander. No longer captivated by the sounds of the birds and the color changing sky, I started thinking about my annual New Year's Day party, less than a month away.

"I'll ask everyone to bring an hors d'oeuvre," I said. "And maybe this year we'll play croquet again." I started making a checklist in my head of where I'd position the furniture and how many chairs I'd set up outside.

Then I jumped to my birthday party in March and a possible going away party in April. Suddenly I was all teary-eyed and feeling very, very sad.

And then Marika gently said, "You know, you're not here anymore."

What a great gift to have someone right there to bring me back to the present moment. Just like that, I realized that all of those emotions were NOT part of the present moment. That, when I came back to the present moment I was truly content, happy, comfortable, and so glad to be camping, in nature, belly full with dogs at my feet.

We spent the rest of the evening playing cards to stay connected to the here, the now. What is.

The next morning, Marika went on a day long birding adventure with a hired guide. As the dogs and I sat around camp, I started to feel that same sadness coming over me. I realized that my thoughts had been wandering again and I needed to bring myself back to the here and now.

I leashed up the dogs and we walked out into the desert where, now, leash-free, they ran and sniffed, digging into rabbit holes, finding stray sticks for fetching. The sky was clear and blue and wide and I breathed in the cool air and stood in the courage of warrior pose, facing the morning sun.

When we got back to camp we sat outside as the cranes began to fly in after their early feeding in the nearby agricultural fields. I heard their sounds first, the invisible but raucous chorus of trilled grawking and honking. Then a string of fast moving dots appeared in the sky. As they got closer the dots became v-shaped patterns ribboning toward me, getting even louder.

I could make out the silhouettes of their 72-inch wingspans, fast-flapping in the air. They circled the shallow ponds in a noisy display, flying low, then around in a circle then low again to land.

And then, just as the sounds seemed to settle over the water, another burst of honking filled the air to the east. The line of dots appeared, fast and close and the honking from the air sparked the honking of the birds below that had already landed. Even from my vantage point a quarter of a mile away, the sounds were almost deafening.

More cranes appeared, as if the noise from the ground had called them and soon my inexact counting reached one thousand cranes. And more were coming, honking, flapping, trilling their calls as the surface of the ponds became a field of solid gray.

 **_HEART SPARKS_**

How do you notice your thoughts?

How do you bring yourself back to the here, the now, what is?

Practice 5:

Letting Go

Letting Go and Letting In

As you begin to focus on your intention and what you want, you'll also notice things in your life that don't support this new thought, this new direction, this new vision of yourself. You'll begin to see what you might be holding onto that really, no longer serves you anymore.

Sometimes you hold on to things. Sometimes it is an old belief that holds you back. Sometimes it is the fear of letting go of what you know, even if you don't really like it anymore.

By identifying what is no longer supporting you or serving this bigger vision that you are beginning to see for yourself and your life, you can begin to let them go.

Letting go is about taking inventory of what is and isn't working in your life. Letting go is stepping back to hear the stories we have been telling ourselves, and discerning if they're still true.

A willingness to let go gives you permission to really ask yourself, Does this thing or this thought or this person support my intention?

Does this thing or this thought or this person fit with this dream I have?

Does this thing or though or person support who I am

becoming?

What am I ready to let go of to create the space for this bigger vision of myself?

One of my clients, Sandy, said that this single exercise helped her realize how important it was to prioritize time for herself.

She created several hours in her day for exercise and more sleep. And she realized how much better everyone else felt when she felt better.

It is an amazing feeling to let go of old stuff, old habits, old patterns. New space opens up and suddenly, anything is possible.

HEART SPARKS

For the next 7 days, I invite you to pause before you make any purchases, accept or decline any invitations.

Instead of deciding on the spot, tell them you need to think about it and you'll get back to them.

And then consider, does it support who you are and who you are becoming?

Why might you say yes? Why might you say no? Are there any 'shoulds' popping up that you might want to let go of?

Clearing the Clutter: Creating Space

Clutter isn't just piles of papers and stacks of unsorted bills. Clutter can be anything you no longer use: trinkets you used to collect, clothes you no longer wear, wedding gifts from a previous marriage.

Not only do these things take up space in our homes, they keep us attached to a version of ourselves that we no longer are. And until we let them go, we cannot move into the authentic person we truly are.

For several years I created artworks from found and recycled materials. I had full drawers and boxes, neatly organized and arranged with all kinds of objects and doodads for my creations. Sometimes a friend would call, asking for some odd item and, sure enough, I had it.

But after two years of not making art, it occurred to me that, not only were all of these things taking up precious space, but they were making me feel bad that I wasn't creating anything.

I kept the things for "just in case" I needed something, but realized that, I can always find them again if I do. (And finding them was part of the fun of it, after all.)

The bottom line was, I was no longer that kind of artist

and so I didn't need to hold on to all of those things.

There was such spaciousness in the revelation. I spent an entire weekend sorting through all of my stuff. I filled four boxes for Goodwill, two bags for trash and even made a pile of some real treasures to give to an artist friend. And yes, I kept a few special items that were just too wonderful to part with.

It was a great feeling to open up the now-empty drawers, to feel the space I had created. Not just the physical space in the drawers, but that new space in my identity.

I loved being able to stretch into the new questions: Who did I want to be now? How did I want to express myself creatively now?

It's impossible to move into this place of transformation if we are living in a space filled with old things, old beliefs, old habits.

The first step toward any change is really examining what we want, because then we can begin to see what no longer serves us. From there we can find the courage and the desire to let those things go, in order to make space for new growth, new questions, new possibilities.

 *HEART SPARKS*

What things, beliefs, habits are cluttering your life and keeping you from being able to ask new questions?

What are you ready to let go of that is no longer serving who you want to be in your life?

From Fallow Fields to Flower Fields

This letting go business is tough. When we let go of something, how do we know something better will come? What happens if it's gone forever?

Whenever I start to doubt, I turn to Nature for assurance. Nature seems to be a wonderful reflection for us humans.

In Carlsbad, California there is a place called The Flower Fields where they grow acres and acres of ranunculus. From March through May, the fields are full with every color of flower: red, orange, yellow, white, pink, even purple, as far as you can see.

But after the season, the farm workers harvest the seeds from the remaining crop and plow the fields down. They fumigate all the beds to be sure to kill everything. And they let the soil rest.

Through the winter the fields are empty, colorless, waiting. In early spring, new seeds are planted by hand, row after row, the workers trusting that the coming year's crop will bloom as colorful and beautiful as the year before.

While previous harvests strongly support the possibility, there is no guarantee. But the flowers certainly wouldn't grow if the farmers didn't first clear the fields.

It's the same with people.

We have to let go of the old to make space for the new. We need to sit in that empty space of fallow fields, allowing our own ground to rest before something new can grow.

A woman in my Virtual Living Room Ladies coaching circle is redefining what it means to be an artist. While she has let go of her youthful visions and expectations of an artist's life, she has no idea what that life could look like now. And she is very uncomfortable with this blank slate.

Because if it's not what she always thought it was, what is it?

She is in the fallow fields. She has plowed the fields and fumigated the beds and now she must sit and lean into that quiet empty space. Maybe it isn't yet time to plant the new seeds. So what can she do? (We all want to be DOING something to move our progress along.)

Well, sometimes the best doing is just Be-ing. Being able to sit with the thoughts that come up, to calm ourselves when we butt up against our own impatience, to dig deeper into our own soil to reconnect with the reason we want to do this thing in the first place.

She will know when it's time for planting. She will know what seeds to scatter. She will know how she wants to bloom.

HEART SPARKS

Do you remember a time when have you been in the fallow fields?

What did you learn from the experience?

How do you stay with the uncomfortableness?

How can the seasons support you and your process?

Floating as Meditation

I am a Pisces, born on the last day before water becomes fire. So it is no surprise that I find deep comfort and joy being in the swimming pool.

I enter from the steps, inching my bare skin into the cool water, then I dive under and in. I get about half way to the deep end before coming up for air, my neck arched back so that my hair is back, off my face.

I dog paddle the rest of the way to the edge of the deep end, then bicycle peddle back, focusing on a different part of my body with each lap, moving, stretching, propelling myself across the water.

Laddy lifeguards from the pool deck, following me up and down the length of the pool. I plunge and splash across the shorter width of the pool and he runs from side to side, barking.

Mabel follows him with her green squeaker toy in her mouth, then drops it so I can toss it in the water. She rushes to the loveseat, steps in and swims to retrieve it, then takes the long way across the pool to come out on the steps where Laddy is usually waiting.

At the end of my aerobic time I slow my movements,

keeping my shoulders under the water line so that I make no waves, no sounds. I move into stillness, standing in the deep end, suspended, focusing only on my breath. When I inhale, my whole body rises, as if levitating out of the water. When I exhale, all of me sinks into the water, up to my mouth until I breathe again, rising.

Eventually I move onto my back and float, my body loose and sure, leaning into the water beneath me. I feel every molecule of the water holding me, supporting me. I wiggle my fingers and snow angel my arms through the water until I can no longer feel where my skin ends and the water begins.

My ears are underwater and I hear myself breathing, slow and deep, in and out. The more air I take in, the higher my body rises, and as I exhale, the water covers my belly and my chest. I allow my whole face to submerge, leaving only my nostrils exposed. And just when I think the water will fill my nose, I breathe deep, lifting, rising, floating.

 *HEART SPARKS*

How do you relax? I mean really let go?

When do you feel held by a power larger than yourself?

When The Only Way Out Is Through

It was advertised as a great family trip, a leisurely four hour, 15 mile kayak on the Manistique River through a wildlife refuge. I had watched the video on youtube of a father and son, all smiles and sunshine as they paddled past trees and the chirping of birds.

Marika and I love nature, love being on the water. We've kayaked many times together, in bays, along sloughs, we even paddled across a stretch of the Pacific Ocean to get to a great birding spot. So we thought, what better outing than to kayak through the wildlife refuge.

The woman at the kayak rental place explained the route. "You'll pass under the Ten Curves Bridge, then in another 2 miles you'll go under the M-77 bridge." She pointed to a spot on the map." That's your last chance to get off the water. After that you're on your own until the put out, 15 miles down."

We eased down the muddy bank and got in the two seater kayak with Marika in the front for unobstructed bird viewing. We pushed off and started paddling. It was so lovely to be on the water, in the quiet, surrounded by the forest of tall, green trees.

We found a rhythm of paddle left, paddle right, gliding, almost effortlessly in the water. We hadn't kayaked together in more than four years but it was coming back so naturally.The river was quiet and slow as we approached the Ten Curves bridge. The kayak floated, barely moving, as we stopped to take pictures.

We followed the lazy turns in the river, steering left, then right, then straight ahead. Marika spotted a kingfisher so we stopped to watch him hover, then dive into the water. Further down a great blue heron fished along the shallow bank, then took flight, his wings spread wide, as we got closer.

We approached the M-77 bridge a few minutes later. The air was cool, the sky clear and open and, after two miles, neither one of us was at all ready to call it quits. We passed the sign welcoming us into the Seney Wildlife Refuge and paddled alongside a pair of wood ducks near the river bank. We followed the curve of the bank, scanning the trees for birds. Suddenly the river narrowed. The low hanging branches of the trees that had barely been touching the water now reached halfway across our path.

We steered the kayak sharply to avoid the branches, then had to quickly turn in the opposite direction to avoid a submerged log. The clear calm water had become an obstacle course of low hanging branches, sunken logs and jagged rocks.

A canoe with two men and a woman appeared with fishing rods. We watched as they guided their boat ahead of us, the man in the back of the boat nearly losing his fishing hat as he limbo-ed under a very low hanging tree.

We followed their path, Marika calling out directions - rudder right, hard left - as we maneuvered around the low tree. We turned a sharp right to avoid another branch and got caught on top of a fat log. We were balanced along the length of the log, but our kayak was completely out of the water.

Before we even had a chance to consider our predicament, the canoers paddled over and pulled us off and into the water. After many thank you's, they paddled ahead and disappeared around the next curve.

Marika continued to navigate, avoiding the obvious ripples in the water that indicated there was something underneath the surface. We got stuck on a sandbar but easily pushed ourselves off with the oars. At one point we got caught against a big log. We couldn't paddle left or right so we let the current turn us around, then we paddled hard against the water to get back on course.

We passed the sign marking the first five miles. Marika looked at her watch - we'd been on the water almost two hours and we were getting hungry. I took two apples out of the dry bag that I was using as a foot rest to give me more leverage as I paddled. We floated and ate, keeping a keen eye out for the path of least obstacles.

We took turns paddling and resting. Marika's shoulders were sore. My hands were cramping. I dragged them through the cold river water, fingers spread, to relieve the tightness.

The map indicated a wide sandy beach just before the half way point where we planned to stop for lunch. We passed several small patches of sand, then saw a wider stretch of beach and paddled to it. With the front of the kayak solidly on the beach, I got out and pulled Marika and the boat out of the water.

We sat in the sand and opened up the dry bag, preparing for a feast. But Marika's ham and cheese sandwich was now a squishy mayonnaisey mess from me stepping on it. She managed to pull one thick slice of ham from the wet mess. We shared some carrots, my leftover chicken tenders, some lettuce, a package of peanut butter crackers and an orange.

Back in the water we found our rhythm, still navigating the fallen trees, the submerged logs, the hidden rocks. The sun was lowering, casting its own shadows on the water so that now we couldn't tell which way the river turned, much less, what was in our way.

We paddled slower, with more precision, ready to act

quickly when we came upon a hazard. I traced the curves in the river on the map, calculating how far we'd paddled, scanning the banks for the sign that would indicate we only had 15 more minutes before we'd see the place to pull out.

"I see the sign!" I said, ecstatic that we had made it. But as we got closer, I realized that it wasn't the sign that we were almost done. It was the sign for the halfway point.

Words cannot express our shock, our disbelief, our incredulous realization that we still had 8 more miles and at least 3 more hours to paddle.

We were tired. We were sore. We were spent. And yet we had no choice. There was no rescue boat to call. No bank to pull out on. There was no way out except to keep going.

"Oh my god, you're kidding me," was all I could say, while Marika kept repeating, "We just have to do it."

We laughed at how ridiculous our situation was. We imagined scenarios where a motor boat would come speeding down the river and tow us to safety. We joked how the rental place never asked us about our kayaking experience or our endurance.

"I have to cry," I said. I needed to release the frustration, to get past the wall I'd hit. The tears helped and after a few minutes I had a second wind.

We paddled steadily for what seemed like hours,

wondering if we would make it to the pick up point before dark. We hoped someone would still be there to pick us up.

And then we saw our canoe friends. It was such a relief to know we weren't alone. They had snagged several of their lures on the logs but had caught two good sized pike, but they were also tired and ready to get off the water.

They stayed close behind us, following our trail around the debris in the water, encouraging us, saying we were looking good, that we were, indeed, gonna make it.

And then we saw the sign marking the 15 minutes to the pullout. We all cheered, keeping our eyes on the banks for the concrete marker. "We're almost there!" I said, as we turned a curve and saw our kayak outfitter guy standing on the shore.

We paddled close enough for him to pull us up the steep bank. We were too sore and too stiff to say much as he pulled Marika and then me, up and out of the boat.

But we did it! We paddled fifteen miles in six hours on a twisted curvy natural river with fallen trees and submerged logs. We didn't give up. Because we couldn't. We had to keep going.

Life is like this, too.

You hit a patch of pain, or grief or uncomfortableness.

It hurts so much that all you want to do is stop. Or turn around. But you can't. Because the only way out of it is to go through it.

If you're lucky, you have someone to help, to get you unstuck, to cheer you on. Maybe you even have someone who paddles along with you.

But ultimately, you have to have the strength and determination within yourself to keep going if you're going to make it through.

Because it's the only way.

HEART SPARKS

Can you recall a time when you had to keep going, even when you wanted to quit?

How did you get through the experience?

How can you use those "survival skills" in daily life?

It's Alright to Cry

I have been crying a lot lately. But that's not why I'm writing this. I'm writing this because, for years, I hardly cried at all.

Like most of us, I've had sorrow and trauma in my past. But instead of feeling it, sharing it and releasing it, I buried it. I tucked my sadness and grief deep and away, convinced that, if I didn't feel it, it would disappear.

My biggest fear was that, if I started to cry, to FEEL my sadness, that I would never stop.

And so I denied it, avoided it, distracted myself with addictive behaviors to prevent myself from feeling any kind of vulnerability. And if something happened in my life that did poke at my vulnerability, I quickly busied myself to avoid confronting any deep feelings.

This "worked" for a long time. And then it didn't work at all.

I was always agitated. Crabby. Needy. I wasn't allowing my body to ebb and flow through ALL of my emotions. Just like the body needs to laugh and sleep and breathe clean air, the body needs to cry. Crying is the only mechanism the body has to release certain toxins and chemicals.

Dr. William H. Frey II, a biochemist at the St. Paul-Ramsey Medical Center in Minnesota, analyzed two types of tears: the emotional ones (crying when emotionally upset and stressed) and the ones arising from irritants (such as crying from onions).

He found that emotional tears contained more of the protein-based hormones, prolactin, adrenocorticotropic hormone, and leucine enkephalin (natural painkiller), all of which are produced by our body when under stress. This explains why we usually feel better after a good cry.

Now I cry for all kinds of reasons. I cry when I am disappointed, when something that was supposed to go one way, turns into something else. I cry when I think about those last precious days with my mom. I cry when my hormones take control of me. Sometimes crying is me hitting a wall of fear or frustration or wanting to give up. Crying allows me to feel all of those things, naming them, and claiming them and then letting them go so I can move past them.

I cry when I am full of joy and gratitude, too. It's like I can't contain it, don't want to hold it in...it's literally an outpouring of WOW! and YES! and I JUST CAN'T BELIEVE IT! Crying is emotion overflowing. It's like the release valve on a pressure cooker, no matter what's in the pot. Crying makes room for even more. Crying is a wet thank you. An Oh My

God without words. Crying is when there aren't even any words. Crying is sweet gratitude. Crying is soggy love.

 *HEART SPARKS*

The next time your feelings poke you and you're tempted to hold back from crying, breathe into the resistance and give yourself permission to feel whatever you feel. Keep breathing into the tightness, allowing your belly to soften, your heart to open, and let those tears roll down.

Trust that you're not going to drown yourself in a never ending tsunami of emotion.

Just hold on, let go and ride those tears to a new way of release.

How Not to Live in the Past

I received an email from a reader asking how she could stop regretting her life and be happy.

Regret is a sign that we are living in the past, stuck in what was, what wasn't, what might have been. Some regrets are small. We feel bad that we forgot to send someone a birthday card. Other regrets are bigger. We wish we had spent more time working on a past relationship gone bad.

The first question to ask yourself is: Is there some action I can take today to change the situation?

In the case of the forgotten birthday, we could still send a card. After all, there is a whole line of Belated Birthday Wishes.

As for the past relationship, there may be nothing you can do to change the outcome. And so you have to find a way to make peace with that regret and let it go.

Shifting our focus to the Now, the Present Moment, is the easiest way to move from that place of regret.

Connecting with our breath and just breathing can calm us into the present moment.

If we are consciously breathing, following our breath inside and then out, we are no longer any- where except here. And in the Here and the Now, there is no past, there is no future. There is no regret.

I suggested to my reader that, every time she found herself 'living in the past' or feeling some kind of regret, to immediately notice it, acknowledge it, and shift her focus to something right here, right now, in the present moment.

It could be watching the birds, or playing with her dog, or smelling some spices in the kitchen. Engaging our senses moves us out of our heads where we get stuck in our old thoughts and patterns.

Saying thank you for something or someone in our present life can immediately shift us into the Now.

Perhaps it's time to write a letter to your past. Acknowledge it, thank it, grieve it, so you can let it go. Then burn the letter, releasing it to the fire and the air.

The more we can "train" ourselves to shift out of the past and into the present, the less often we will feel regret.

HEART SPARKS

Is there something you continue to ruminate on with regret?

How can you make peace with it to let it go?

What can you say 'thank you' for?

Blessing the Openings

Native Americans have a tradition called The Sacred Smoke Bowl Blessing, often called "smudging," which is a powerful cleansing ritual. Herbs and incense are burned with the idea that smoke attaches to negative energy and, as the smoke clears, it takes the negative energy with it.

Smudging is not the process of eliminating or killing anything, but simply the shifting of energies so that there is a balance of positive and negative.

Here is an opportunity for you to bless and balance this new space you have created in yourself and in your life.

What you will need:
some incense (sage, cedar and sweet grass are most commonly used in traditional smudging)
two pieces of paper
matches or a lighter
a big glass of water (just in case)
a well-ventilated room or a place outdoors

a metal baking dish or non-flammable bowl

Light the incense and slowly take a few breaths to relax yourself and come to the present moment. Feel the space inside of you that you have created. Notice what it feels like, if any emotions are still attached to that space of letting go.

On the first piece of paper, write what you are releasing. It can be a single word, or a paragraph that sums up what the clutter in your life symbolized.

Crumple the paper into a loose ball, place it in your burning bowl and carefully light it with a match. Watch the smoke and flames rise up, carrying that which you have released up into the atmosphere. Follow your breath, inhaling and exhaling with awareness.

As the smoke clears and the paper disintegrates, consider what new things, ideas, traits, inspirations you'd like to come into your life.

Hold this vision in your heart as you write it on the second piece of paper. Again, it can be a single word or a paragraph. Be clear. Be concise. Be sure.

Crumple this paper into a loose ball, place it in your burning bowl and carefully light it with a match. Breathe deeply, inhaling and exhaling as you watch the smoke and flames rise up, carrying your new visions into the atmosphere. Feel the space you have created, inside and outside.

Breathe into this space. Make it holy. Make it yours.

Practice 6:

Imagining

The Magic of Imagination

As children we know no boundaries to our imaginations. We pretend we are super heroes, we draw crazy planets and six-eyed monsters. We invent machines that can clean the world. We don't know that these things may not be possible.

But then we grow up and we're too busy with the rest of living to spend much time pretending or imagining.

But tapping into our imagination, that place of unbounded freedom, is a wonderful tool for getting unstuck, for envisioning what we cannot fathom with our rational adult minds.

Pretending is especially helpful when we feel stuck about something. We know we want to do something, but we can not figure it out with our minds.

But what if we just pretended....

One of my coaching clients wanted to go on a weekend vacation to San Diego by herself. Recently divorced, she had never traveled alone and was feeling stuck in the fear of the unknown. Who would she talk to? Who would keep her company? What if she got lost driving around?

OK, I suggested, let's pretend.

I asked her to imagine herself walking along the beach, her favorite place. She was immediately able to transport herself, walking in the sand with bare feet, feeling the cool breeze on her face, in her hair.

She said she felt free.

She imagined herself meeting people on the beach, striking up small conversations with other travelers. She envisioned herself with her morning coffee, sitting in the sand, just watching the waves roll.

She realized that, by traveling alone, she wouldn't have to compromise about where she ate, when she ate or anything she wanted to do. And suddenly, the idea of traveling alone became an adventure that she was looking forward to.

Imagining is a powerful tool even if you aren't stuck on a particular thing.

Simply allowing yourself to daydream, to drift into another world without boundaries or limits can free your thinking and open you up for so many other things.

HEART SPARKS

Imagine you are 7 years old.

Not your former 7-year old self. No, imagine, you, right here, right now, are 7 years old.

You have no job. No responsibilities. No big worries on your mind.

School is canceled, you have enough money to have fun and you have the entire day to yourself. What would you do? Where would you go? Who would you spend the time with?

Chances are, after you've reveled in this fantasy, you will feel more relaxed, more open, maybe even a little more playful.

Permission to Dream

I had dinner the other night with a friend who, for several years, and many reasons, has stayed in an unfulfilling marriage.

But now, she is taking the steps toward divorce.

While she knows it is the best choice for her, she is freaking out about the future.

How will she support herself?How is she going to live?What will her life be like if she is not married?

And when she asks these questions, there is so much panic and anxiety in her voice that she freezes.

I suggested she change the intonation of her questions so that they are more like open-ended wonderings that don't require immediate answers.

I asked her what her dream life might look like twelve months from now. Without hesitation, she began to describe a cozy house and she would paint all the walls whatever colors she wanted. Her whole face lit up as she shared her dream of this community house filled with books and space for people to just come and hang out.

And then she stopped. "But it's not practical," she said.

And I asked her, "Does it have to be practical right now?"

My friend doesn't anticipate being on her own for another 6-12 months. And so, I suggested, maybe she doesn't need to be practical right now.

I suggested that this time right NOW could be an opportunity to begin to dream, to imagine all kinds of possibilities for herself in this new life. I offered that she could simply entertain her joyful imaginings so that the space opens up for what she might really want to create for herself. And that, eventually, that imaginings would reveal something practical.

"You mean, give myself permission to dream?" she asked.

And she realized it had been so long since she had.

 ***HEART SPARKS***

When was the last time you gave yourself permission to dream?

Is there something that keeps you stuck in practicality?

Would you be willing to open up to what might be possible beyond practical?

Do you even have dreams?

One Hundred Sticks

In many of my workshops we play a fun brainstorming game that I call 100 Sticks. We stand in a circle and pass around a plain wooden dowel. Each person has to name one thing about it that describes what it is. We usually go two or three times around the circle, pushing the limits describing what the stick is: slender…smooth…about two feet long…brownish..

And then I ask, What ELSE is it? It's not a stick it's a…. conductor's baton, a sword, a pool cue, a baseball bat. We pass the stick around the circle again, this time offering up ideas of what else the stick could be. We go several times around the circle until the obvious answers have all been said.

And that's when the game gets fun. And powerful. We've exhausted all of the easy answers and now we get to push past what we know, and open up to what else it could be.

It's a little exhilarating to come up with something new. And it's frustrating when you get stuck again.

Sometimes, watching how another person holds the stick will spark an idea. Sometimes just turning your body, shifting the dowel in your hands, will inspire something. And usually, the most creative answers come when you don't think you could possibly come up with another idea.

This same exercise works when we are stuck with something in our lives. We've been thinking and thinking and thinking but we can't come up with any new options or ideas.

Playing this game, exploring all of the obvious choices, plans, and possibilities, will help open you up to what else might be possible.

HEART SPARKS

Begin by writing everything you know about the thing you're stuck about.

Brainstorm all of the steps necessary, everything that you know, everything you've already considered. Keep writing until you can't think of anything else. And come up with two more things.

Then, on a new page, continue brainstorming, asking: What else do I know? How else could I do it? What else might sound good? What else? How else? Where else? Why else? Who else…

Again, keep writing until you can't think of anything else. And come up with five more things.

Let the answers be wild, impossible, just crazy enough that one of them might actually work!

Do this with a brainstorming partner or in a group for more powerful openings.

Name It, Claim It, Let It Go

We all have dreams. The cryptic ones that come to us at night. The ones we've been imagining since we were children. And the ones that appear when we are in deep connection with our hearts. The thing is, if we keep them to ourselves, our dreams cannot manifest into reality.

When you have a strange sleeping dream, doesn't it become clearer when you tell someone about it? And don't you get all giddy when you talk about your childhood dreamings, even if they are too silly to really happen?

Sharing our dreams is the most powerful way to turn them into possibility. Giving voice to want we truly want gives the vision energy. Telling someone else alerts the Universe that we really mean it. Envisioning one detail at a time brings it closer to reality.

And hearing our own voice proclaim our deepest dreams brings us face to face with our own role in making it happen.

It is no longer a secret. And there is the power!

Maybe you envision a beautiful home with a wrap around porch and you have walked through the rooms a hundred times in your mind, running your hands across the furniture, choosing the colors of the walls, even imagining who is standing around in the kitchen, sharing a delicious meal with you.

Maybe you have a vision of your ideal partner. You know what they look like, smell like, if they speak with an accent. You imagine how their skin feels and how you feel when you are with them.

Maybe your dream involves travel and adventures and exotic foods.

On one hand, it's important to engage in these fantasies because they awaken the imagination, which sparks an opening in our heart. And it's important to keep the dream alive in your awareness, with a daily affirmation, a dream altar, or a poster on your bathroom wall that you see every morning and remember.

At the same time, it cannot become an obsession.

You need to maintain a balance between asking and receiving, between action and waiting, between knowing and letting go.

And you have to remember that it is not your job to figure out the how of your dreams. Your only responsibility is to stay focused on the why, the heart, the essence of what you desire.

Why do you want this?

How will you feel when you are doing this?

How will living this dream serve others?

Our dreams guide us in the direction of our heart. But as we get closer to manifesting something, our perspective will change, and we must be willing to let that original vision become something else, something that will better serve us, even if it's not at all what we, in our feeble little minds, had imagined.

I am in the midst of manifesting my own big dream to live at the beach where the air is cool and clean. I am making plans, setting dates, shifting my work life to support this dream. There are moments, days, even, where I have a very clear picture of how I am living my life there, how my whole world will open up, and how much more deeply I will do my work. And I share my excitement and plans with my friends.

And then I get stuck in the financials, the logistics, the details. And I change my mind about HOW I'm going to do things. My heart fills with doubt and regret that I have changed my mind, yet again, and I wonder, what will my friends think. But you know what? They think I'm human. They think I'm creative for coming up with so many ways to do this. They think I'm brave and inspiring for taking this giant leap into my dream.

A friend recently reminded me that dreams are fluid. They are not frozen in time exactly as we originally imagine them.

Our dreams are always shifting, changing, seeking their own level, like water.

Remembering this brings me much peace and comfort. Of course I'm going to change my mind several times as new information comes to me. Of course I will waver between excited and fearful. Of course I won't know how it all unfolds until it happens.

And so I keep flowing with the energy of the dream, keep bobbing in the waves of change and always, my dream on the horizon, getting closer and closer.

HEART SPARKS

What are you dreaming?

Write it down.Not in your private journal.

Write it out in the open.

Draw it in big bold colors on a giant piece of paper and tape it on the wall in your bathroom where you (and maybe other people) will see it everyday.

Call a friend and share it, out loud, with them.

Find an object that symbolizes your dream and carry it in your pocket.

And check in with yourself: How insistent are you that it should manifest exactly how you've imagined it?

How can you let go of all of that and allow your heart to lead you to what you really love?

Getting Un-Stuck: A Lesson From Paper and Glue

One of my favorite things about my work is using creative exercises to help my students and clients learn more about themselves.

Thinking our way to a solution often keeps us stuck. Engaging our hands, our senses and our imaginations is a powerful and surprising way to problem- solve, to move forward, to get un-stuck.

I recently taught a collage class for kids at a local art gallery. After showing the group several styles of paper collage, they were invited to create their own masterpieces.

Most of the kids dove right into the project. They loved the permission to tear pictures out of magazines. They cut shapes from patterned papers, crumpled gold and silver foils and glued textured rice papers over images to create interesting layers.

But there was one 10 year old boy who really struggled because this wasn't a 'first do this, then do this and it should look like this when you're done' kind of project.

All around him, the other kids were already ripping and cutting and tearing. One girl even announced, "I have a plan!"

But he just stood there, not knowing where or how to begin. I asked him if any of the samples interested him. He pointed to the one of a man surfing on a giant fish, where different images were glued together to tell a new story. I told him that I understood his frustration, that, when I had made that collage, I had no idea what it was going to be, and that I had just started with the background and eventually, I found the other pieces.

I suggested that he just start cutting stuff to warm up his cutting muscles and see where it took him. His silence said he wasn't sure, but he grabbed some patterned papers and began cutting random rectangles and gluing them on his blank white paper.

When I checked in with him again he was positioning an astronaut and a candy bar on top of the patterned background but he wasn't happy. He walked back to the supply table, touching different papers and textures. You should have seen his face when he got an idea. He glued silver foil over the patterned background and suddenly his astronaut was floating in space. He added gold stars to create a galaxy. He held up his masterpiece and he was smiling, ear to ear.

I thanked him for sticking with it. I applauded him for just starting, not knowing where it would lead him. And I hoped that he would remember this the next time he felt stuck and didn't know how to begin.

 ***HEART SPARKS***

How do you get un-stuck?

Consider making a collage of images that catch your eye or that tell a new story.

If You Can Dream It...

"Imagination is more important than knowledge." Years ago my father gave me a coffee mug with that Albert Einstein quote on it. My father is an engineer, a mathematician, and so this gift struck me as odd, because it seemed like it was the opposite of my father's logical approach to life. But he explained that, as an engineer, it's not enough to know what he knows. He has to be able to predict what might happen, or what part might fail based on the information that he has. And to him, that was a kind of imagination.

Imagination can also mean daydreaming with limitless abandon. Imagination can be about seeing the possibilities of your dreams as if they have already manifested. Imagination can get you excited about what's truly possible for yourself and your life.

One of my clients has always dreamed of having his own art studio. He's a very visual guy so when I asked him about his dream studio space, he described how one wall would be lined with shelves for all of his art books, that his table would be right by the window with the best light. His voice got so excited as he talked about all of his paints and brushes, and how he already knew how he would decorate the space.

Some people call this visualizing. I prefer the word imagining, because it invites all of your senses in to play. Some people aren't able to "visualize." But there are other ways to imagine.

Maybe just thinking about how having your own studio space would FEEL is how you play in your imagination. Or writing your name with a fictitious address is a way to imagine yourself in a new space. You can fill a bulletin board with pictures of what you will have in your studio when you move in.

The more you play in your imagination, the more you will begin to believe that your dreams really can become reality.

So do you have vision, an idea, a dream in your mind? How detailed have you really gotten? How much time do you spend daydreaming about it? Have you imagined really BEING there, DOING this thing, LIVING this life you're dreaming?

 *HEART SPARKS*

PART 1

Assuming you have all the money, experience, skills and talents that you need and want, what would your dream day look like?

Where do you live? It can be a real place or a fantasy location.

Who do you live with?

Begin with waking up.

Take yourself slowly through your entire day, writing down everything that would be a part of your dream day. Notice everything in great sensual, vivid techno-colored detail.

Be sure to engage all of your senses, including smells, sounds, taste, touch....notice the light, the temperature, the time of year. Notice your mood, your breath, your outlook on the day.

How does this thing that you REALLY want to be/do play out in your ideal day? Is it even a part of it?

Take your time. Have fun! It's YOUR ideal day!

PART 2

After you've written down your entire ideal day, step back and breathe. Now read it out loud, proclaiming to the Universe that YES! This is what I want!

But, remember, your dream will not manifest exactly like you've imagined it. The details will most likely be very different. But the feelings of what you want will be astonishingly similar.

So go through each sentence, each paragraph, each scene and distill the important words, the essential parts.

What words repeat themselves?

What details are non-negotiable?

What are the deepest truths about this vision?

Write these down on a new piece of paper and then, once you have extracted the essence from your writing, burn your original vision.

Yes, burn it. Tear your pages into tiny pieces and light the words on fire. Watch the embers dance and the smoke rise, as your vision becomes one with the air.

Allow the Universe to receive your request.

Let go of all expectations and preconceived notions of how it will manifest. Focus, instead, on the essential parts, the way you want to feel.

They are magic clues to your deepest WHY.

When Gratitude Becomes Gladitude

People will tell you that, if you're feeling sad, depressed, hopeless, the best thing to do is make a gratitude list. To find simple things that you are grateful for, to shift your attention to what you do have, to what is working in your life.

But often, when we are in this dark place, it's hard to conjure a list. And when we do, the things we come up with seem too simple and silly. Like a roof over our heads, a perfect cup of coffee, that our phone didn't fall in the toilet.

We make these lists but we don't often feel great waves of gratitude. And that's OK. Because just thinking about some positive things in your life will create a shift. Because suddenly you are aware that not everything in your world is horrible.

Eventually you'll be able to really feel the simple joys of saying thank you. You'll realize that having a roof over your head keeps you dry and cool and comfortable. That when you enjoy a perfect cup of coffee, nothing else has your attention. And when you think about how inconvenienced you might have been if your phone had gotten wet, well, this is when gratitude becomes gladitude.

Gladitude is saying 'thank you' from a deeper place in your heart. Like you really mean it. Because you do.

HEART SPARKS

Start a gratitude list. Every day, find a scrap of paper and write down something you are grateful for in that moment. Then throw the paper away.

Do this every day this week, at the same time every day so that it becomes a ritual.

This is not about keeping a gratitude journal or finding the right notebook to write in. This is about the gratitude itself, which is why I encourage you use scraps of whatever paper you have lying around. Once you write your gratitude and acknowledge it, you no longer need to keep the paper.

Finding a Hole in the Fence

I was talking with my client, Sue, about her dream to create a dog sanctuary. She envisions a many-acred facility that rescues dogs, finds them homes and, for those unadoptable ones, provides great care and companionship.

Sue clearly sees a loving staff working with her, organizing successful fund raising events, and the joy that this work brings her.

I invited her to make a list of the steps she can take now to keep this vision alive. While she came up with a wonderful list of self-care actions, I was surprised that there was nothing on her list that had to do with dogs.

When I asked her about it, she said, "When I think about volunteering at a local rescue place, I know I would just want to take all of the dogs home with me. And I can't do that. So I can't volunteer."

Sue had created a black and white, all or nothing situation in her mind and it was keeping her from doing the work she loves.

I asked her if she could imagine herself being with the dogs at a local shelter, giving them love and attention. I asked her if she could imagine being a part of an organization where she was learning how such an organization worked. I asked her if this would outweigh the fact that she couldn't take them home.

She tilted her head to the side and laughed. "I suppose I could do that." And then she laughed again, this time at herself, for letting that all or nothing thinking stop her from doing what she loves.

Often, when we have a resistance to something, we hear our reactive thoughts and stop. But what if we approached the resistance with curiosity, with a question, "How and why is this holding me back?"

We can explore this with a visualization.

Imagine you are walking on a path and, in the distance you see a fence. From far away the fence seems to be blocking your way.

What is the fence made of?

How tall is it?

What is on the other side?

As you get closer to the fence, you see that it isn't impassable. Maybe you see that it is flimsy, or fallen down in places. Maybe there is an opening in the fence that you can easily climb through.

We don't have to tear a fence down to get past it. And we

don't have to let it stop us, either. What if, instead, we explored it, looking for a way around it. What if we could find a hole in the fence to go through?

Sue didn't suddenly stop wanting to rescue every dog. But she no longer let this stop her from helping a hundred more.

 *HEART SPARKS*

When you think about your dream life, where is your biggest resistance? What feels like the largest obstacle?

What is the fence that is holding you back?What is on the other side?

What does the fence look like?

Are you willing to explore it, have a dialog with it?

Can you find a hole in the fence?

Practice 7:

Taking Action

Ready Set Action

Action doesn't mean you have the whole plan laid out. Action is taking the one next step in the direction of your dreams.

Action is saying yes. It is deciding. It is making the choice to align your thoughts and behaviors with the bigger vision you have of yourself and your life.

You can dream all of these great possibilities in your head but if you only fantasize about your life, you'll never be living it.

Saying thank you, being grateful for what is working in our lives, is taking action. Changing a habit is action. And sometimes, doing nothing is the perfect next action step.

Just listen in, let go and continue to follow the direction that your heart is leading you.

How Courage Begets Courage

I have my mother's body, from the two chins and small hands, to the renaissance curves and pendulous breasts. My belly, round and firm at the same time, a small waist compared to my buttocks that are wide like all the women on her side of the family. I have the same thick thighs and narrow feet, and the pinky toes that curl under the other toes.

My mother chewed antacids as far back as I can remember. I could always find a white box of peppermint CHOOZ gum in her pocketbook, on her headboard, in the glove compartment. For years my mother swallowed her anger, her grief, her feelings of losing control.

I am much better at expressing myself - crying, yelling, feeling my feelings and letting them go. And still, I have the same reflux issues that she did. The ones that eventually turned into esophageal cancer and killed her.

And it scares me to death.

I sometimes cough up gastric juices in the middle of the night if I don't sleep with the head of my bed propped up on risers. I am taking the same medicine that my mother was on (in smaller doses) and not eating after 6 pm. I try to avoid chocolate and spicy foods and sugar, all triggers for the acid. And still, the reflux wakes me up from a dead sleep.

And each time my food comes back up at me, I think of my mother, how she felt full after eating a quarter of bagel, or three little peanut butter crackers. How she tolerated the experimental procedures to blast the cancer with pellets down a tube in her throat when radiation and chemo were no longer an option.

I know that the power of my fearful thoughts can't be helping the situation. And that stress is a major contributor to reflux. But I have been too afraid to do anything about it.

My friend Liz has a family history of colon cancer and she's been avoiding a colonoscopy for several years. When we got together a few weeks ago she told me she had finally made an appointment, just to get it done. To know. And the results came back-no cancer. No pre-cancer. No need for another test for five years. She was ecstatic.

I was so inspired by her courage that I finally made an appointment with the gastroenterologist, the same doctor who first discovered my mother's cancer. I told him I wanted an endoscopy to know what the inside of my body is really doing. I wanted to hear him tell me that I don't have Barrett's esophagus, the wearing away of the lining that is a pre-cursor to cancer.

I wanted him to tell me that if I just lose weight, the symptoms will go away and I will live a long and healthy life. I wanted him to reassure me that, in this particular case, I do not have my mother's body.

He assured me I don't have any alarm symptoms. That losing weight will, indeed, alleviate the reflux. And I had the endoscopy just to be sure. I got the same all-clear results that Liz got and am already experiencing less symptoms.

HEART SPARKS

What scares you that you have been avoiding?

What courageous act can you follow through on?

Allowing the Unfolding

I absolutely love teaching art classes for children. The kids are open. Willing. They are happy to dive into whatever we are making, often without even knowing what the final product will look like.

Sometimes I show the kids samples so they can see different interpretations of the process. But not always. Because often the kids will think theirs has to look exactly like the sample.

I recently taught a book making class to group of 8-14 year olds. I intentionally didn't show them what the finished book would look like. Instead, we began by brainstorming nouns and verbs and adjectives.

The dry erase board was filled with words like hot dogs, zebra, flowers, puppies and run, play, eat, dance and smelly, tall, fat, purple.

Together, we combined some of the words into silly sentences, like 'zebras dance with purple puppies' and 'smelly flowers run with smelly hot dogs. Then the kids wrote their own words and made new sentences.

Once the kids had their content, we began on the

construction of the actual book. It involved a lot of measuring, folding and line drawing.

One twelve year old girl kept asking why are we doing this step? What are the lines for? Why do I have to measure this?

I asked her if she'd be willing to NOT know, and maybe feel excited when she figured it out. I asked her if she could just trust the process.

She thought about it for a minute and then said yes.

She seemed to relax as she drew the lines across her pages, then wrote her word phrases in the top, middle and bottom boxes she had created. When we finally got to the step of cutting the lines between the phrases, her face lit up. "OH!" she said, "I get it now!"

All around the room the kids were discovering that, by cutting the pages in thirds, the story would change, depending on which part of the page they turned.

After class I asked the twelve year old how it was to just follow the steps without knowing why. She smiled and said she was really glad I didn't give it all away.

Sure, sometimes we need to know why we are doing something. We need to know what's next, so we can be ready.

But NOT knowing can be equally valuable. Not knowing gives us a chance to be surprised, delighted, and present in what we are doing in the moment.

Several years ago a friend and I were having lunch and I was bemoaning that I couldn't see how I was going to do some big thing with my life.

She said, "How about if it's ok that you don't know? How would it be if you just let it unfold?"

Her words struck me so deeply. "I would LOVE that!" I said. "But how do I do that?"

Of course she laughed, because it is all about NOT doing.

For the past few years, I've been practicing this letting go, allowing things to unfold. Being OK with not knowing.

And it's been amazing. Just taking one step at a time and then, just like the girl in my class, experiencing such delight when suddenly I see how it all comes together.

HEART SPARKS

Where in your own life can you let go and not know?

What do you need to let go of in order to embrace this idea of allowing the process to unfold?

Speak Up, Sing Out, Share Your Authentic Voice

One of the many things I've learned these past few years is how powerful the voice is. When we add sound to our movements, to our thoughts, to our sentences, the energy expands. And yet, so many people are not comfortable making sounds, speaking up, being heard.

Listen around you to how quietly some people speak, especially when they are talking about something personal and important.

Growing up, so many of us were told to Be Quiet. Many of us were told we had bad singing voices, so we should just mouth the words. We were encouraged to be seen, not heard. And we have accepted these statements as truth, and have settled back into shameful silence.

Until today.

If we want to be heard, we must learn how to be comfortable using our voice.

We must believe that our words, our ideas, our perspectives are valuable and worthy of sharing. And that we have a right to speak up, speak out, even sing out.

Several years ago, a Living Room Lady shared that she used to love to sing. But her third grade music teacher told her she was off key so should just mouth the words. For all those years in between, she kept quiet, not even singing in the shower.

And then one night, after a powerful Living Room Ladies gathering, she attended her granddaughter's birthday party and got up and sang karaoke. And she loved it. She couldn't believe how fun it was and how much she had missed singing all these years.

When we don't use our voice, we lose our voice, both literally and figuratively. Maybe we are more prone to sore throats or coughing. Maybe we feel like we are never heard. Maybe we don't tell our own truth, for fear that we won't be accepted.

Recently, in a different Living Room Ladies group, I asked each woman to write an affirmation that would guide her toward the more joyful, more authentic life she desired.

One woman wrote, "I am honest about who I am and not afraid to voice it."

This single sentence suddenly gave her permission to speak up for herself. And with practice, she will even be comfortable doing it.

 **_HEART SPARKS_**

How can you get more comfortable with your voice?

Perhaps you can begin with just sighing an audible sound when you exhale. Notice if your sound is quiet, or fully supported by your outgoing breath.

Making silly sounds with your voice also opens up the channels. Singing gibberish silliness is a great way to reconnect with your voice. Find a young child and sing with them–they will certainly not judge you.

Even if you think you can't sing, do it anyway.

Creating the vibration in your throat will reverberate into your heart and your entire body. Try it. Feel it.Add words to the sounds.Sing an affirmation.

Raise the volume so you are really heard! Having the support of strong breathing will also help you sing more in tune.

Sing it loud. Sing it proud. Sing it long. Sing it strong.

Begin to claim your voice and all that you are here to share!

Sitting In Stillness Opens a Heart

Life is funny sometimes. We tend to avoid what we need and want the most. And then circumstances happen and we are suddenly faced with exactly what we weren't able to give to ourselves.

Leaning into it, accepting it, can be a challenge.But when we are able to be grateful for the experience, magic can happen.

Several weeks ago I tweaked my back (again) and spent five days resting, moving slowly, doing virtually nothing.

I couldn't walk the dogs or do the laundry or run errands. I couldn't sit at my computer for very long. I couldn't do any of the things that I usually do to distract me from my heart work.

But it was such a gift, really, to have my body step in for me and give me what I most needed– time to let go and do nothing.

Because it is in this quiet space of stillness that we can choose to release the struggle and begin to ask, what do we really want.

The weeks leading up to my tweaked back had been very stressful, emotional, and challenging and I was feeling especially agitated, restless, uncertain. I had big choices to make and I had no clarity about anything.

I knew that what I most needed was to let go of all of the struggle and just step away from myself and create some space.

But I was too caught up in it all to do that. And then I tweaked my back and had all the space in the world.

In the stillness of not working, not housekeeping, not care taking, I could feel myself letting go of the struggle.

I was taking deeper breaths. I journaled. And I got very clear about what my heart work really is.

Not surprisingly, as soon as I named and claimed it, emails appeared in my Inbox with opportunities to do that work. (Really!)

And I was standing straight again, walking my regular pace. I felt a lightness in my body and so much excitement in my heart for these new possibilities.

Struggle is hard. Stillness can be uncomfortable. But, for me, leaning into that quiet space is the only way to let go and discover what my heart really wants.

 **HEART SPARKS**

How do you create and enjoy stillness in your life?

How does your body get your attention?

The Lesson of the Bamboo Tree

Recently, Elizabeth, a client I've been working with for almost a year, was complaining that, even with all of the great work she's been doing, she was still stuck in her dead-end job. "I've shifted my attitude, I'm focusing on my intention, envisioning my dream job. Why haven't I found it yet?"

I acknowledged how frustrating it can be not to see obvious growth and change. I reminded her that all things come in time, just not necessarily on our time table. And I told her about the bamboo tree.

The bamboo tree is one of the strongest plants in the world. It is also one of the fastest growing plants in the world. Some species can grow as much as 4 feet in 24 hours.

But when a bamboo is first planted, there may be no visible growth for the first 3 -5 years.

This is because the plant is establishing its root systems so that it can support itself when it begins its phenomenal growing spurts.

I reminded Elizabeth that she is establishing her own strong root system so that, when she makes this big shift in her life, she will feel strong, stable, supported.

We may not think anything is happening, we may not see any progress. But that's what building a foundation is all about.

When we plant a new seed in our lives, we don't know how long it will take to grow. But if we want it to bloom we need to water the seed, give it light and love and tend the ground around it so that it has the best possible growing conditions.

And we need to have patience and faith that, like the bamboo, it will, indeed grow.

 *HEART SPARKS*

What seeds have you planted?

How do you tend them?

How do you maintain patience as you wait for them to bloom?

What We Get When We Give

We've all heard that it is better to give than to receive. Giving and doing for others is the fastest way to get out of depression and woe is me. The selfless act of doing something for another human being or animal or nature or cause can fill the heart with pure wonderfulness.

And the best part is that, when we give, often what we receive in return is even bigger.

Last week I had the honor and privilege of facilitating a workshop at the local senior community center that my Dad enjoys. My mother used to love going to the center for the activities, the people, and the sense of community. I wanted my workshop to honor my mother and her time at the center and so I shared some of the tools and practices that helped her maintain a positive attitude, despite her health challenges, age and circumstances.

I invited the attendees to draw a big heart on their papers and write inside of it all the things they love. Then each person stood up and read their list out loud, filling the room with so much positive energy.

We talked about how, when we choose to focus on the

things that bring us joy, our bodies don't ache as much, we forget about the negativity in the world and we don't feel so alone.

We talked about paying attention to what makes us happy and living with an attitude of gratitude. Then we went around the room, sharing something we are each grateful for. We talked about how good it feels to be able to do something for someone else. And even though we would sometimes rather be able to do something ourselves, letting someone do something for us is a wonderful gift that we can give another person.

It was a real pleasure to work with these brave, wise folks. We had a lot of laughs and we all learned something about living from the heart. But more than that, it was such a gift to be with people who knew my mother, who came up to me and shared a memory of her, of how much they liked her and admired her and missed her.

I was surprised by the experience. Standing in the middle of the room that was filled with everyone else's gratitude and love, my own heart was truly overflowing with gratitude and all that I had given and more: it was filled with all that I had received.

HEART SPARKS

How do you give?

Do you take care of someone in your family?

Do you belong to a committee?

Do you tithe a portion of your earnings?

Do you donate money to a favorite charity?

Do you volunteer your time and special gifts?

What do you receive from your giving?

Leap and the Net Will Appear

It's such a wonderful concept, this leaping. It's all about risk and faith and letting go and pushing aside all of the monkey voices in your head that talk you out of doing some big, scary thing and just going for what you really want.

Although the phrase "Leap and the net will appear" is sometimes attributed to an unknown Zen source, it is, in fact, a quote by American naturalist John Burroughs.

I first heard the phrase in the song, "Right Outta Nowhere" by Christine Kane.

"Right outta nowhere

You open your heart

And let go of everything

And you're going somewhere

And all you need to know

Is that you're free to go...

Dream and the way will be clear

Pray and the angels will hear

Leap and the net will appear"

The song encourages us to open our hearts, let go of any

expectations and trust that the wide open space will hold us, guide us, support us.

Leap and the net will appear reminds us that, if we want to do something beyond our comfort zone, we have to take that first, unknown, scary as hell step. We have to leap with the faith that we are on our true path. And that some net, some larger force, some divine energy is guiding us. And that if we do not fly, we will be held and supported as we fall.

Leap and the net will appear is not about knowing how it will turn out. It's not about having all your ducks lined up, with more than enough funds in your IRA, just in case.

It's about trusting that this thing that calls you, that your heart is guiding you toward, will support you and teach you and bring you to a richer, fuller more authentic way of being you.

Sometimes leaping is very scary. Sometimes leaping seems impossible. Sometimes leaping is the only possible next step.

HEART SPARKS

What does leaping look like for you?

Taking a cooking class?Submitting your artwork to a gallery?

Applying for a new job? Training for your first marathon?

What one thing can you do today to get this leaping in motion?

What To Do When Nothing Is Working

It happens to all of us. We get a great idea. We're motivated. We take the first step toward what we want and we're cruising. We feel excited. Rejuvenated. Like this thing could really happen!And then something doesn't turn out the way we had hoped or expected. And we land in a pile of doubt.

Sound familiar?Did you start the year thinking this would be the year of the Big Change?

Maybe you're ready to find a new career or to pursue that dream you've always said "someday" about.

You made your list of everything you wanted, opened your heart to the universe and said, "Bring it on!"

Maybe you even found a great job to apply for. You revamped your resume and aced the interview. But you didn't get the job.

You feel defeated and so full of doubt that you wonder if you are ever going to live the life of your dreams.

If you are standing in that space of ready, and unknown, it can be very uncomfortable. What do you do now?What do you do next?Is this even going to work?

Change is not linear. And big changes don't usually unfold the way we envision them. Often, when we are in the midst of big changes, it seems like nothing is happening. It seems like the opposite of what we want is happening.

And so the real question is, how do you move through these challenging times, when it seems that nothing is working the way you want?

Sometimes, the best thing we can do for ourselves is to pause. To completely stop rushing and doing and striving and simply BE exactly where we are.

This shift in rhythm can open us up to opportunities to notice our accomplishments and revel in how far we've come. Instead of pushing further, we have a chance to breathe into the present moment and check in with ourselves.

What do I really need right now? What do I really want to do?

Maybe you need a nap. Maybe you need a cool glass of water. Maybe you want to call a friend just to tell them you're thinking of them.

When we're always focused on what's next, what else, what more....several things can happen: we don't appreciate what we've already done, we don't appreciate what we already have, we often don't realize how tired we are, and we don't honor what we really would rather be doing or not doing.

 *HEART SPARKS*

I invite you to try a new phrase. Instead of asking What's Next, consider What's Now.

Bring your conscious awareness to this moment, where are you right now.

Breathe into your belly and follow your breath in and out, noticing its pattern, its rhythm, its presence in your body.

And ask yourself, What's Now?

Ask yourself, in this moment, how can I best support myself?

What do I need right now?

What's Now?

Do this often enough and you will notice a shift within yourself. You may be less cranky, more patient, more compassionate with yourself and others.

By slowing down and paying attention to the here and the now of life, you'll begin to notice all kinds of magic.

Cause For Applause

I was listening to Annie, one of my coaching clients, share some of her weekly successes. She had cleaned out an entire closet, paid her bills early and had scheduled a long-overdue manicure for herself.

She was moving so quickly through the list that there was no pause for honoring her accomplishments. And when she did pause, it was to counter the success with a "but I didn't...."

I had to stop her. I gave her a big shout out for each of the successes. And I asked her to join me in a big **WOOHOO! YAY! I DID THAT!** celebration.

And then she said, "Wow, I didn't even realize how much I'd done."

Often we are so focused on plowing through our to-do lists that we don't honor the work we're doing. We don't take the time to celebrate our successes. We don't breathe in how good it feels to accomplish something.

No wonder we still feel overwhelmed with what else we have to do.

And when we counter what we have done with a but, (yes,

I did that BUT I didn't do the other thing), we are negating ourselves, dishonoring our success, sabotaging our own power.

I asked Annie to pay attention to this pattern and, whenever she hears herself say 'but' to stop and take the opportunity to celebrate what she DID do with a big YAY! She liked the idea.

Later, in our conversation, she started to go down that but road and immediately stopped herself mid-sentence. She didn't YAY, but I could hear her smile.

HEART SPARKS

How do you celebrate your accomplishments?

How often do you honor what you've taken care of, what you've done for yourself?

How often do you give yourself a big high-five YEAH???

A Different Kind of New Year

Wednesday evening marks the beginning of Rosh Hashanah, the Jewish New Year. One of my favorite concepts about the holiday is the idea of starting with a clean slate. All past mistakes, hurts and transgressions are forgiven.

But, unlike other religions, it isn't God that you ask forgiveness from. God forgives everything.

Instead, we seek out those who we have judged, or offended or hurt and we ask THEM to forgive us.

We begin anew because we have owned our actions and genuinely said I'm sorry to the person who we hurt.

Another ritual of the holiday is Tashlich, meaning cast off. We go to a body of water and, using bread crumbs, we symbolically cast our sins into the moving water. Again, we are claiming accountability for our actions, forgiving ourselves and letting go. And in doing so, we can move into the new year without the burdens and regrets and mis-steps of the past.

It is tradition to gather with family and friends and share a delicious holiday meal on Rosh Hashanah. My family always enjoyed a many course meal: gefilte fish with salad, chicken soup with kneidels, my mother's sweet, tender brisket with crisp, roasted potatoes, string beans with almonds and a sweet carrot tzimmis, and honey cake, my father's favorite, for dessert.

It's also a tradition to eat apples and honey for the New Year. These sweet foods symbolize the sweetness we wish for ourselves and our loved ones in the coming year.

These are wonderful, powerful rituals. Saying I'm sorry.Making peace with the past. Letting things go. And opening up to the joy, the sweetness of what is and what else is possible.

HEART SPARKS

Perhaps you'd like to incorporate some of these rituals into your life this week.

Maybe you will call a friend, or send a note and say you're sorry.

Maybe you will take some bread crumbs to your neighborhood park and forgive yourself with each toss.

Maybe you will gather with loved ones and indulge in all the foods that taste like love.

Maybe you will dip a slice of apple in honey and open to the sweetness of your life!

Luck Has Nothing To Do With It

"Good luck and good fortune are about choice, not about control. When we are clear that we are choosing our lives, and when we understand that making choices is not the same as managing the outcome, luck and fortune find us every time."

~ Molly Gordon

Luck is winning the lottery. Or making all the green lights. Or getting a level camping spot with an unobstructed ocean view.

Living out a vision that you've been dreaming about for years is all about intention, effort and taking actions that may mean you give up one thing in order to get something else. And it has nothing to do with luck.

When I tell people that I'm living and working in my motorhome two blocks from the ocean, often their first response is, oh, you're so lucky. Or worse, they respond with envy.

I want to sit down and tell them how long I've been working for this dream, how much I've invested in my business to get it where it supports me virtually.

And I want to offer them hope and a starting place so that they, too, can begin manifesting their own biggest dreams.

The first step might be to take the energy that you're investing in envy and jealously and use it to get clear about what your own dream is for your life.

Never mind the voices that say, "I could never do that."

Instead, ask, "what if I could, what would I really want to do?"

You have to have a destination first, if you're going to create a road to get there.

You may not know HOW you're going to do it, or when, but if you begin with the vision, the desire, the intention, you have the most important piece of the plan- your WHY.

Your WHY is your heart speaking. It is your deepest truth, your guiding light, and it is often connected to how you can best serve others. Your WHY is the unbending compass that will keep you moving forward on your path.

The where and the how and the when will probably change, but your WHY will remain constant and strong, so that, when you are faced with the challenges of making it happen, you can come back to the heart of the reasons WHY you're sacrificing, WHY you are working so hard, WHY you want to do this big thing.

And you'll take the next first step toward making it happen.

HEART SPARKS

What dream is tucked in your heart?

Are you ready to take it out into the light and claim it?

What is the next first step you can take?

Thank You's!

I have been wanting to write this book for many years. I could see parts of it - the structure, the themes, I even had the names of the seven practices. But I wasn't ready.

I am so grateful for the people in my life who encouraged me to keep at it, to do what I love, to follow my dreams:

My mother, Beverly Davis, who I miss everyday, for nurturing my creative spirit and wanting to read everything I wrote, and for buying me the hardcover Writer's Market every year when I was in college to show her support.

My father, Sol Davis, a feminist before his time, for raising me to believe that I could be and do anything I wanted to.

Marika, who is more than my family, my soul-sister, my traveling companion. She pushes me to do my best work and be my most human.

My friends who are my family, who love me and believe in me, no matter what, and help me remember myself when I forget: Sheila Levine, Maggie Feldman, Annie Volpe-Fetzer, Lynn Terleski-Katz, Judy Hulden, Carey Avery, Debbie Wohl Isard, and Frannie Walsh. And my community at Desert Song Yoga, who I OM with every Thursday morning at 10:30, even when I am not there on my mat.

Thank you to the women who have come to my workshops and retreats and allowed me the gift of sharing these practices, trying them out and learning so much from you in the process.

And thank you to the Living Room Ladies, the ones who met in my actual living room, and the ones who were so brave to meet online, in a video chat. What an honor it has been to do such deep and heart-filled work with each of you.

Thank you to my blog readers who invite me into your inboxes, who send notes saying that something in that week's **Heart Sparks** resonated with you, made a difference, was exactly what you needed to read in that moment.

Thank you to my many Mac clients who have supported me all of these years, doing work that I love.

Thank you to my teachers, in and out of the classroom. I have loved words since Mrs. Sorkin, my second grade teacher, had us cut out pairs of construction paper hands to learn about homonyms, two words that sound the same but are spelled differently. I am forever grateful to her for sparking my love of language and story-telling. And thank you, Tracy Trefethen, a writing teacher many years later, who encouraged me to trust myself to tell the truth, to write deeper. And thank you, Patti Digh (rhymes with pie) for leading me back to my writing practice.

Thank you to the Life Coaching teachers at SWIHA, where I learned that good coaching is about asking really good questions.

Thank you to my online mentors whose words inspire me enough that I wanted to share them:

Michelle Woodward: www.michellewoodward.com

Molly Gordon: www.shaboominc.com

Christine Kane: www.christinekane.com

And thank you to the artists who share their work on the pages of the e-book:

Valentine Janice McDonald, www.janicemcdonald.com

Sewanee Sunrise Rebecca Roberts

Serenity Ileen Miller, www.leenieworld.blogspot.com

The Last Days of Summer Barbara Bagan,

www.artandaging.com

A Gaggle of Geese and Friends, Julie Schoen

Tears Wendy Schneider, wendyschneiderart.com

Full Circle Miranda van den Heuvel, www.createandart.com

Adversity Lisa Rough, www.SacredCircleCreativeLife.com

Sometimes I Send Myself Flowers Stacey Beth Shulman

And thank you to my book team for their incredible enthusiasm and support during the process: Laraine Herring for always reminding me that the shortest distance between two points is a Davis; Crys Williams for the initial "Pinch" that got the ball rolling, Sheila Levine, Frannie Walsh and Debbie Wohl Isard for their great feedback as first readers, and Anoki Casey, my graphic designer, for turning Barbara Bagan's watercolor painting, *The Last Days of Summer*, into a most delicious book cover.

And thank YOU for reading all the way to the very end.

Resources

Rainer Maria Rilke, Letters to a Young Poet.

"I've Gotta Crow" from the musical production of Peter Pan, lyrics by Carolyn Leigh

The Flower Fields in Carlsbad, CA: www.flowerfields.com

lyrics from "Right Outta Nowhere," Christine Kane, www.christinekane.com

Get the audio recording of the breathing meditation at http://www.sparktheheart.com/mp3/breathing.mp3

Join the Heart Sparks Community at www.sparktheheart.com

Order more books at amazon.com